Peace Flowing Like a River

PEACE FLOWING LIKE A RIVER

Thoughts of
Bishop Kenneth W. Hicks

BY

Bishop Kenneth W. Hicks

Compiled and Edited by T. T. Tyler Thompson

Cover and Text Photos by Cat Todd

PHOENIX INTERNATIONAL, INC.
FAYETTEVILLE

Copyright © 2010 by Kenneth W. Hicks

13 12 11 10   4 3 2 1

Designed by John Coghlan

Inquiries should be addressed to:
Phoenix International, Inc.
17762 Summer Rain Road
Fayetteville, Arkansas 72701
Phone (479) 521-2204
www.phoenixbase.com

Library of Congress Cataloging-in-Publication Data

Hicks, Kenneth W. (Kenneth William), 1923-
  Peace flowing like a river : thoughts of Bishop Kenneth W. Hicks / by Kenneth W. Hicks ; compiled and edited by T. T. Tyler Thompson ; cover and text photos by Cat Todd.
    p. cm.
  ISBN 978-0-9824295-3-2 (alk. paper)
  1. United Methodist Church (U.S.)—Sermons. 2. Sermons, American—20th century. I. Thompson, T. T. Tyler. II. Title.
  BX8217.H53T46 2010
  252'.07673—dc22

2009054337

To my wife, Elaine, my parter in ministry, life, and love

and to our daughters Linda and Debbie,
and grandchildren Kiley and Spencer.

Seek peace, and pursue it.
—Psalm 34:14b (NSRV)

CONTENTS

PREFACE

It is an honor for me to have been entrusted with the opportunity to organize and edit this book authored by a man who commands a great deal of respect among the various communities in which he lives and works. He has spoken and still speaks all across the United States, and his important impact on the efforts of Peace Ministries has had positive influences reaching around the globe.

Though I knew of Bishop Hicks when he first came to serve in the episcopacy in my home state of Arkansas and later admired his writings in the *Arkansas Methodist* newspaper, it wasn't until he retired from his two 4-year terms as bishop in both Arkansas and Kansas that I had the pleasure of knowing him as a friend.

Upon retirement Bishop Hicks returned to Arkansas in 1992 with his gracious wife, Elaine, and they chose to attend and continue to serve as Christian mentors to the congregation at Little Rock's Pulaski Heights United Methodist Church, my home church. The two of them have added an enormous dimension to our congregation's ministry, and we are all the richer for knowing, serving, and fellowshipping with them.

Since 1992 you would hardly realize that Ken Hicks has actually retired. He is always serving on one board or another, presenting a special seminar or study series here or there, or flying off somewhere to speak on a panel, preach a series of sermons, or preside over some national, regional, or other such prestigious meeting or convention.

And if it's not one activity of the above, either he or Elaine is recovering from another health challenge that has tried to put a roadblock in their path of life. But when that has happened, they each push through the pain of healing and rehabilitation with a lot of prayer and trust in each other, appearing once again in our presence with smiles and comments to us that always ask "and how are you doing?" Very special people, indeed.

Since Ken and Elaine retired to PHUMC, he has routinely been most benevolent with his time in teaching Bible Studies and other short courses on various subjects that interest him, most specifically peace and justice issues. And I have taken as many of his courses as possible and enjoyed them immensely. Shortly after I took my first course with him, I asked him if he had ever written a book. He said that he hadn't, to which I said that I thought that he should. His comment to that was, "Well, isn't that nice of you to think so." I literally have pestered him over the years to write one until, I dare say, sometimes I fear he hated to see me coming down the hall of the church.

Finally, I thought that I should give up asking him because I didn't want to alienate him—when in the spring of 2008 at the beginning of a Lenten study course he was teaching, Bishop Hicks came into the classroom with a satchel full of old columns that he had written over the years for the Arkansas and Kansas Area Conference United Methodist newspapers. Also included were a number of poems that he has penned over the years. He told me, "See what you think you might be able to do with these." I was so ecstatic I could hardly say a word, but I couldn't wait to get to work.

Even though the words herein were largely written two to three decades ago, Bishop Hicks has reread all of the included pieces and only modified a few lines to make them relevant today. That gives you an idea as to how timeless most of his thoughts were at the time his pen originally hit the paper and how they are still important lessons for us in the present.

A word about the photos on the cover and within these pages: they were taken by Cat Todd, a young lady who is also a member of PHUMC and a recent graduate of the University of Arkansas at Little Rock with a degree in mass communication with a minor in photography. I really appreciate her allowing us to use her images to enhance the bishop's text.

Bishop Kenneth W. Hicks—he is the person I think of when a person is sought to lead the singing of "Let there be peace on earth, and let it begin with me."

I hope you enjoy his thoughts.

—T. T. Tyler Thompson

INTRODUCTION

Peace Flowing Like a River as the title of this book is prompted
by the recollection of the river near my boyhood home in southeast
Kansas. To think of the Neosho River conjures up memories like
those of a movie recalled long after being viewed. The images are
of real people and real events: swimming with neighbor kids, or
alone with Grandad, and the Fourth of July community picnics on
the shaded bank of the river with the grounds abounding with
neighbors. Grandfather and I fished and rowed the old green row-
boat up, down, and across the river setting or checking trotlines or
just getting to the other side for any reason.

During the dry 1930s our stock well went dry. My father and I
hauled water with the farm wagon laden with barrels drawn by our
faithful farm horses. Dad would guide the team so as to find the
familiar spot where the water would be deep enough to minimize
the reach between the water and the barrels. As I recall, the river at
that spot had a cleansing, satisfying sound as it sloshed into the barrels bucket after bucket. The river was never dormant, but alive. The
famished livestock would quickly consume much of our load upon
our arrival back home. The river was alive, thus able to give life.

Peace does flow like a river. It must be cherished and experienced. Peace is not something to be arranged, but something to
give as a witness of our having experienced it.

The pages that follow describe a riverbed of experience that was
offered as a ministry to the best of my ability. There was movement,
though I saw it sometimes "filling the barrel." I wasn't always cog-
nizant of such meaning, but looking back to younger days as a much
younger minister, I now know there was movement empowered by
God's mission. Presence and Incarnation have meant for me ministry that is not primarily programs or activities. Rather, ministry is
Presence of a Lord whose nature we see modeled by Jesus.

The poems were first composed for the sake of my own spirituality. They are not the best of poetry. That is obvious. They are descriptions of the flow—the current at a particular time. I hope the articles and essays provide some insight as to where I have been. For the most part they are drawn from "Bishop's Corner" articles prepared for the Conference newspapers where I had the pleasure to serve. I wish I had been more faithful for the accounting for dates of specific entries—but the time frame is 1976 to 1992, and the places were Arkansas (1976–1984) and Kansas (1984–1992).

It is my belief that we must become the Peace we long for. One thing Jesus has taught me is that God has long struggled to have a human form. That's who Jesus is, God as human likeness. His Presence (whether realized or unrealized) is within the human heart waiting to experience the river of life with us. Can you feel it? His Presence is like a living current, a flow of love that invites us to share Creations and His work of peace for all.

—Kenneth W. Hicks

CHAPTER

1

Bless the Beasts . . . and Nature

An Old Black Dog

An old black dog joined me on the beach today.
We scarcely knew each other.
We met but yesterday.
But something within us wanted to take a hike,
     so off we went together.
We were friends of the beach,
     friends of the dampened air.
There was enough we liked together
     to make us brothers.
When we stopped to rest under rays
     of scarce infrequent sun,
     we talked instead of walked.
He rested against my leg and let me talk.
My pay to him was some rubbing on the head;
     a few strokes on the neck.
The gentle scratching of my hand on his stomach
     really sealed the bond.

In a while, a half an hour or so,
     we said, "so long."
He wanted to go back home.
I hope he went home with more than we started.
I remained and contemplated God,
     then I went home, too, with more than when I began.
                    KWH

God's Creative Hand

Lord of summer sunshine,
The veins of your creative hand
    are seen in roots, stems and buds.
A bird song says something of God
    if only we understand.
Life lives on life to the extent that
    death has more purpose than we know.
Why should the worm be food for the bird;
    the bird be food for the cat?
Why should our body be received again by
    the open earth,
Unless there is continuity, trust, order and meaning?
                                KWH

To My Granddaughter

Dear Kiley,

A terrible accident has happened near Valdez, Alaska. In water that has created and energized life in so many forms in its primal state, ten million gallons of oil have spilled from a tanker that hit a reef. The captain, who evidently has a serious alcohol problem, was not in control of his vessel and an unqualified officer was in charge.

The spill now covers over 3,000 square miles. Loons encased in oil cannot fly, otters with fur pasted down are freezing, salmon are endangered, and the long-term effects cannot be assessed except that they are *long* term. It is assumed this vast ocean area will probably manifest signs of this desecration for years, maybe forever.

Kiley, I'm sorry that I am of a generation that has built its values on a system that ravages the future for you and your brothers and sisters of the Creator. I repent of this happening for I am a part of the human family with whom God has promised to be a good God. We have forgotten that the earth is God's. Of God the Psalmist says, *"The heavens are thine, the earth also is thine; the world and all that is in it, thou hast founded them"* (Psalms 89:11).

As one of God's creations, I am part of the human family with whom that covenant is established. Thus, I cannot be faithful without repentance for what has happened.

I repent that the church is indifferent to the extent that we allow the travesty on the environment to occur instead of crying out with the loons that cannot fly, the otters that cannot swim, and with who at the killing of Abel by Cain demanded, "What have you done?"

We have done something terrible to your future. It is occurring over the world. Acid rain, the burning of the rain forests, the advancement of the greenhouse effect, the polluting of the waters of oceans and streams.

What your world will be like fifty years from now, I cannot imagine, because like a locomotive without brakes, we have placed a travesty in motion that will not be reversed in the foreseeable future.

Kiley, my prayers are becoming simpler. I pray now, "God, bless the children of the earth, and the beasts of the field and sea. Forgive our trespasses against them. And forgive religious folk who sing 'This is My Father's World' while ravishing the earth of its creative powers and beauty."

My dear granddaughter, I, your grandfather, do not have a completed salvation yet because of what we, the dwellers of this time, have done to blemish the covenant God has made with God's people.

To you, and all children, the salmon, the otters, the sea lions—the whole balance of nature containing God's grandeur, I repent of my generation's ways and our values that demean the future and which are robbing you of the treasure which belong to you on this, God's beautiful globe. We, who are now adults, could put in place the policies which would save the future if we would, but as of now we lack the will. We are devourers not only of the present but also of the future.

I love you. Try always to care.

While in Scotland

Scottish air so cool
    on this July day;
Scottish sky so blue
    on this July day;
A setting for scenes where Highlanders grew.
Those bold hills where castles stand
    as aged sentinels
Brooding over cruel hard memories
    mingled with triumphs,
The times when freedom won over dungeons,
    goodness over evil,
    beauty of spirit over malice.
The beauty of the gentle hills seems
    as creation in motion—mounds of soil
    rolling as waves toward the sea.
There is exhilaration in this rugged people
    who have stood firm,
        died bravely,
            yet still endure.

                    KWH

Is There Strength?

With wind blowing on this April afternoon
I am transported to a world
In which growing rhubarbs and jonquils
Are the rule instead of the exception.
To ride a bicycle against this brave April wind
Tests out the horsepower of my legs,
The muscular nature of my wind.
Maybe I don't have power to meet the
        challenge of summer.
I thought it took strength and courage
        to last the winter.
But summer takes strength of a different kind.
It's "want to," courage and power.
    I want to go to the world's far ends.
Is there strength?
I want to set in motion everything that can grow.
Is there strength?

                        KWH

If you want to, you can make me clean. Mark 1:40

Springfever

I've got Springfever, sure as the world.
It makes my eyelids droop.
The flowers peak through the tomb of earth
As if to surprise the world with so much
 we did not plant, nor design.
It's there, as a gift.
We neither hold back nor bring to pass
 most of earth's best.
It's a gift, given in its own time.
We merely see it, if indeed we can,
 or if we are prepared.

The blue martins have returned.
For some it seems they have been here before.
They scout around to see if anyone has prepared
 for their coming.

I had a dog once. His name was Corkie.
 Or maybe it was Corky.
Anyhow, he was the kind of pal who always seemed
 to need somebody.

To sit in spellbound awe of Spring;
To behold that the best of nature is neither
 brought to pass nor held back,
  but it comes as a gift.
     KWH

Hands of Deep Power

Transparent blue hovers over the water.
It, at this moment, has brought with it
    a transparent stillness;
A stillness you can see as well as hear.
If you try, you can feel it too.
Reach out. It's there.
Is this like God?
There are times when you can feel what has no feeling,
    Hear what has no sound,
      See what senses say cannot be there.
      But when there is awe, you know the presence of beauty.

That pelican, those ducks, the screeching kingfish;
they are part of it too, to remind you that you aren't alone.
If God cares for them, how much more He cares for us,
His daughters and sons.

That plane off yonder—
Man has made his birds to fly higher and faster.
But they also make more noise, more mess,
    and endanger more life by far.
The beauty of a duck on the lake, or in flight
    is that it is a duck.
A human being has to take hold of life deliberately;
Take hold of life's design if he is to be beautiful.

The blue grandeur of the lake is possible because
    beneath are the depths.
The substantive depths, upheld by
    the open palms of the lake's hands;
      therein lies the key to God.

God, help us to be aware of the depths of your nature
    like the strong lake bed beneath the surface
        upholding reality.
Grant me the gift of having adequate depth
    that makes possible the witness of holy grandeur.
Don't let us escape the knowledge that underneath,
    deep down, life is upheld by the open, giving,
        supporting hands of your deep power.
            KWH

Hope Resides in the Higher View

On a recent Saturday morning after a grueling week of meetings, appointments in the office, Elaine led me out into the backyard to look at growing things. Also, we were looking at some things that aren't growing, probably as a result of the hot devastating summer last year. We were saddened to see that one of our dogwoods just isn't taking off. We were disheartened to see that it doesn't appear that it is going to make it.

We broke some of the twig branches, most of which were brittle. Just as we were deciding it would have to come out and be replaced, our sight went on up to the top of the tree. To our amazement there is a sparse but beautiful array of blossoms scattered through the uppermost branches.

Whether or not we are able to save the tree remains to be seen. The important thing is we had made a judgment that the tree was dead by looking at the lowest branches. When we lifted our eyes we saw evidence of life and beauty.

You would be surprised what that did to our day. It even gave me renewed interest to tackle the pile of letters and materials that awaited my attention.

Too often we do the same thing with life that we did with the tree. The evidence or the experience close at hand seems to spell doom or at least discouragement. The higher view is, many times, the one whereby hope is restored.

The high view, the long view, is the one that contains hope. The signs of life at the top make us think that perhaps with some special care the tree might pull through.

How many times we make faith decisions by the content of one Administrative Board meeting, one sermon, or one struggle. You can't decide worthwhile matters by the number of blossoms on the low branches. Lift your eyes to the high places, even "to the hills whence cometh my help."

Jesus must have looked higher than Gethsemane or Golgotha. He saw something others did not see, and when He did, what He saw was God. Incidentally, we are going to try to save that tree. It's the possibilities that pull us on to see what extra care, extra love can do.

I suspect that such an attitude could transform a church. And if the church really believes that, who knows, it might transform the world. What do you think?

I Believe That God Does Not Will the Suffering and Poverty of Poor and Oppressed People

Loren Eisely tells of observing one summer a sunflower growing on top of a boxcar. It grew from a green shoot to a flower, then to a ripened pod of seed unnoticed, unappreciated, and unuseful. Then one day an engine came along, hooked onto the boxcar, and moved it into a train of cars. Off went the sunflower, blowing in the breeze. Surely it would not stand the pressure of the jostling and the wind. But alas, as it moved away with increasing speed, the pod began to dissipate, and sunflower seeds were being scattered along the way. The flower would soon be a nonsurvivor. But the seeds were being scattered. Is this not the way of Christian discipleship? Was this not the way of Christ? What dignity! Where is such a church? Where are such Christians?

I believe that God does not will the suffering and poverty of poor and oppressed people. I believe that God does not want anyone, including women, to be second-class citizens. In fact, I see evidence that Jesus in His ministry acted in aggressive ways to dispel both of these myths as blasphemous.

If we have health, let us use it responsibly. If we have wealth, we have a special burden of accountability that goes with that blessing. We should acknowledge our own imperfection as a person or a nation rather than point the accusing finger toward those on whom society has turned its back.

"Thou shall not kill" applies to a Jew as it does to a Palestinian. We have no more right to kill our political enemies than they have to kill whomever they kill. And yet, even American leadership cannot get beyond seeking peace by preparing for war. What is the matter with us? As I read of Jesus weeping over Jerusalem he was not weeping so much over the sins of the common people as he was over the misdirected, legalistic, judgmental, unloving structured lack of Grace.

We are supposedly a nation with moral leadership and religious freedoms, but the most vigorous struggle regarding public education is whether or not to require prayer in school, which is already everyone's privilege who wants to pray. How about teaching children to learn, think, and read?

This evening I have just finished watching a television program on which an advocate of the "New Right" stated that it just may be that the nuclear bomb is a product of the providence of God and that deprivation and poverty are largely the result of lack of prayer and faith on the part of those victims of same. Recently it was in the news that someone exclaimed that the defeat of the Equal Rights Amendment was an act of intervention on the part of God. These points of view are not part of my understanding of Christianity. When, like the sunflower, seeds are sown from the pod of Christianity, shouldn't they be of love, mercy and grace, not condemnation, self-righteousness, and judgment.

Viewing Life in the Context of Eternity

Vacations are mixed blessings. Oh, the extra sleep is nice. To awaken leisurely without the pressure of appointments and meetings is a treat. But, being in Colorado does strange things to a person's system. Altitude has never bothered me, but this time, for some reason, my innards acted in peculiar ways. My first jog made me sick; a hike at 10,000 feet the next day left me invigorated. I'm hungry and sleepy at odd times. The usual is experienced in unusual ways. I even dreamed that I was invited by Henry Fonda to help him sail a two-man vessel from someplace in Africa to England. We almost collided with a motorboat while leaving the dock—end of dream.

One of the great benefits of the high country is to regain a sense of distance and appreciation for the creation drama. One is put in touch with things on a trail at 11,000 feet above sea level, gasping for breath, as nowhere else.

What a vacation does for me is to help identify the pieces that are important to life's wholeness the remainder of the year. A piece of scripture from the paperback Psalms in *Today's English Version* reads differently in the heights.

I'm eager to put the pieces of insight and renewal together into another year of life. I hope I can retain the memory of distance, height, and the struggle for oxygen and distill them into worthwhile attitudes about life, its meanings and goals. One thing a dose of nature provides is the feeling that we really could manage the goings on in the world more effectively if we were to pay more attention to the ways of nature.

For example, if the political shapers were to assemble at the summit of 14,000-foot Long's Peak or on the rim of the Grand Canyon to consider the problems confronting us, wouldn't their judgments be affected by a sense of proportion and responsibility, and maybe shaped somewhat by eternity itself?

Some of the views I have seen lately, some of the strange formations provided by the Creator, the smallness of my existence against the reality of eons of time, make pride in drawing out our enemies seem an act unbecoming of civilized people. What is worse, our actions verify the precarious fragility of our own existence.

A Fig Newton stolen from one's lap by a mountain ground squirrel while taking a swig from the canteen; cheese shared by a Ptarmigan bird beside Loch Vale at 10,000 feet, with Andrews Glacier reflecting into the lake, would surely leave Capitol Dome dignitaries with a feeling that God and God's time have the last word. We can, if we share His extended view of things, assist one another for a brief spell in the sharing of His Grace. But we are the fragile ones! May God be merciful if we multiply the fragility by a sterile vision and compassion. I ascended and was promised the peace of God. I descended and was handed the foolishness of human pride time and again.

My time in the high country and my return to the low country made me know that the only prayer is PEACE WITH JUSTICE. I suspect that the Almighty feels more deeply about this to date than we do.

But the frogs will croak, the clouds will form, the river will run past our cottage, the grass snake will slither, and September will come even after the warheads have had their day. Someone will find a sign, a cross, a baptismal font, or a poem that signified "there were those who believed in the Highest."

Of Menageries and Congregations

I often wonder about what makes the difference in churches. Some congregations seem to have clarity about why they exist, who they are, and exuberance about being in relation to one another. Other congregations seem to be in continuous disunity while reflecting some kind of assumed authority to be on the outs with the denomination, the pastor, and/or each other.

Our house seems to attract pets like flies to honey. But the similarity ends there, and individuality is demonstrated in most un-Christian ways. One cat doesn't like the food service, but will insist on feigning hunger only when another cat who likes the food really wants to eat. Old Whootch, our Methodist cat, is easily intimidated and withdraws from the food dish whenever another one decides to take over. Url is one who turns up his nose unless his particular menu is available. Shad will come around when no one is looking, eat his fill, then act as if he is above the whole mundane process when the other cats are acting hungry. Then there is Sneakers, a little hairy dog who has her own place, has been given individual attention, and is amply nourished; but upon passing by the cat dish, without turning her head a degree, will send out a slender pink tongue for a cat morsel. And she won't miss a step in her trot. You have to look fast to see her.

Those animals are not a congregation. They are an accumulation. Trying to dish up something they will all be satisfied with is a lost cause. They have no intention of finding unity. They are who and what they are. We love them all. But each day when they go out it is up to them whether they want to come back or find another home. The only way we can cope with it is to care reasonably, insist on some limits, and appreciate their differences to the extent we can. So far, they seem to sense that they have been received and are given attention.

Where did I get off of congregations and onto pets? I'll have to let you make the connection. As with our neighbor's cat named "Bobtail," this must be short.

We Weave a Fragile Web

I was in Dallas recently chairing a meeting of the Peace with Justice Committee, the title of a special program of this quadrennium. The magnitude of the task before us causes the adventure to be on the order of dropping a grain of sand in the Sahara.

The plane returning me home was delayed due to mechanical problems of some kind necessitating a return to the terminal for attention. I decided to obliterate the delay by dozing off, mixing in a little reflection on the day.

My thoughts turned to an evening last summer when I turned on the light on the patio. There, fastened to the eave of the house and stretching down to the lilacs was a beautiful spiderweb glistening in the light like a silver aberration just short of three feet in breadth. In the center was a spider presiding over a world all her own. As I approached there was a scurry as if to express warning to me and fear for the spider in case I did not heed.

Keeping my distance, I basked in a moment of wonder to behold a little world apart from my own. It occurred to me that, for the spider, this wonder of creation so delicately designed was her universe. I represented the possibility of destruction. What the spider could not know, or so I think, was that her creation was something I could never duplicate. Moreover, the truth of the matter was that both of our worlds are really quite delicate; and each in our own way was experiencing the fragility of life and the fact that the most beautiful of creations can be swept away in a stiff breeze of happenstance.

There was a brief experience of enhancement in the realization that her universe was little less vulnerable than my own. Her concern for continuity could express itself only by weaving a web of existence which was of value, not for what it did, but for the beauty it was. If, perchance, the web might catch a morsel to perpetuate that tiny life, it was her world as my world is mine. Each of us should be what we are and do what we are meant to do with what the mind of creation has implanted for our use.

The next morning our household was saddened to discover that the woven universe was gone. There was no sign of the presence of exquisite beauty just hours before.

The spider had experienced the holocaust of obliteration somehow. And yet, maybe in the bushes somewhere preparations were being made to create again, to build a new world that would briefly bear testimony again to intricate possibilities worth beholding by some gigantic eye.

My ruminations about Peace with Justice in an hour or so of tormented delay recalled the spider and her web. How much more secure is my world than hers? Gigantic human eyes peruse a world begun in beauty and contemplate the precarious reality that holds the power to sweep away the future; or, should our souls be right, to preserve the design because life is sacred.

Whether it's a breeze, a swinging branch, or a bomb, it is the world of somebody or some thing that is daily on the line. The spider was asking for the same thing as you and I, peace with justice.

The Tides of Change May Sweep You off Your Feet

Elaine and I recently went to Florida for a meeting of a section of one of the agencies I chair. As one whose life has been spent inland, I am fascinated by the ocean. I understand to some extent Jacques Cousteau's fascination for the sea that approaches compassion.

Each day I looked in the paper for the time of high and low tides, not because it meant anything to me as to involvement, but because of the marvel of order and regularity expressed by that part of nature that is the sea.

As God and divine law move the currents and tides of the sea in keeping with the intention of creation, I'm reminded that the same creative law provides the currents on which the actions of faithfulness flow in and out of the ocean of human experience. I believe that our lives can bear witness to that flow. I believe that our lives can move in rhythm to the deeper movements of God's intentions.

One evening as a blustery wind was coming in off the gulf, the waves were rather vigorous. They would sweep upon the shore, sometimes causing me to scamper beyond their reach. But I was looking for shells and anything else interesting that might be swept out of the depths for an inviting eye to discover. As the current wave receded to its rest in the deep, I decided to follow it into the recession to capture something I saw. I scurried after the wave, searching the sand.

While my attention was absorbed in the possibility of treasure as my eyes searched the sand previously covered by water, I neglected to take into account the incoming wave which caught me square and wet. As I scrambled to my feet to leap for dry land, I had nothing but experience and wet jogging clothes for the effort.

My reflection on the event tells me that to pursue the tides of change always carries risk. Our lot is to cooperate with the rhythm of God, to be willing to look for the new and treasured, but always to know the changeless laws that are present. If you don't want to get your feet wet, stay away from the water.

A Costly Trade

Recently, after being gone for several days, we picked up our little dog from the kennel. We asked that they dip her to kill fleas. After about a week she began to have eye trouble. A few days ago when we got up we found that one eye was swollen shut and the other was partially so. Elaine took the dog to the vet. His diagnosis was that in dipping her, the kennel attendants must have let her head go

under, something you are not supposed to do. The result was a deep
eye infection. On examination the sight was gone in one eye. The
prescription was a shot of something and eye drops of two kinds
every hour. He will see her again shortly to determine if the sight
in the sightless eye is returning and if progress is being made. She is
doing better and progress is evident, but the verdict is still out on the
sightless eye.

The trading of sight for fleas is a costly trade, one which we wish
we had not done in such a perfunctory manner. But in other areas
of life we do it all the time. Take religion for instance. We often
accept legalism and miss grace. We often hurry to apply judgment
and miss God's greater love. We see faults up close and miss the
greater concept of vision and value of human life. We stress maintenance and miss religion.

One of the insoluble conflicts Jesus had with the religionists of
his day was His constant emphasis on the long view in the face of
His adversaries' short view. His opponents traded sight for fleas. Jesus
was aware of the fleas that persist in human personality, but He was
constantly urging the use of sight. Referring to the Pharisees in
Matthew 15, He admonished the disciples to "Let them alone; they
are blind guides." Their emphasis was upon fleas. They had lost their
sight of the true nature and values hidden in life.

Back to Sneakers, our dog. We were so concerned about the fleas
that it didn't occur to us she might lose her capacity to see unless
care was applied. What and where are the fleas in our life, in our
church, and how much time and emotion do we exert on the small
things? Our capacity to see life as it is and as it should be in each
other, the world, and ourselves is a spiritual stewardship. In fulfilling
that wonderful capacity to have an eye for the real and the possible,
we have Christ as our model. Let's be concerned about the fleas,
but Christians can't afford to go blind looking for them.

The Sociological Heat Goes On

The hot weather is taking its toll on growing things. Trees and
bushes are showing premature signs of dormancy and death. There

is another kind of heat that needs to be resisted. I guess I would call it sociological heat—the heat of events and attitudes offered up by a world in transition. Kids are going off to college and the costs are terrific. The costs of conducting life, staying in the farming business when crops are stunted, the perplexity of the unsettling new surrounding circumstances we do not understand, the problems of renewing our educational system, the prevalence of drugs, and the international weapons race are but examples of sociological heat, a list that could go on and on.

How do we plan for growth and life amidst the heat? When the heat is intense, even artificial sprinkling and irrigation won't do the job. Spiritually speaking, we need the real thing, don't we? As the old hymn goes, we need "showers of blessing."

Some suggestions, particularly for our church, are as follows:

1. Let us plan as people who are "resurrection" people. God is with us. He hasn't brought us this far to leave us. Let us plan in our church what we wish and intend to have happen. Let us set goals that give evidence that we are a "resurrection" congregation. The life of Jesus Christ must be made evident.

2. Let us plan for evangelistic outcome. This means that we will not just plan for maintenance and continuance. We will plan for mission. We will do such intentional planning not for the sake of morale, but because God is intending for us to grow and flourish.

3. Let us plan as "covenant" people. This means that we will be a congregation which knows we are not a church unless we care for one another. Our intentions for the coming year must reflect the fact that we will strengthen our relationships. Each person who comes to our church for ministry will feel the nourishing strength of God only as we demonstrate it in solidarity with one another as people called by God.

4. As we enter another year of opportunity for our church, let

us honor those who have gloried in the creation of the
church you attend. There are always times when the occasion arises for us to doubt and to be tempted to bail out.
That's when the heat is getting to us. People have lived, sac-
rificed, and now live in memory so that the church in
which you worship could be there.

Yes, the heat is on. It's hard to keep things alive, but the means are
present for us to blossom and grow.

Be Still and Know

I'm sure you have noticed the quietness of early morning. There
are different kinds of quietness that are really quiet. The first is the
quiet of the early morning hours when it seems that only a portion
of the world is present, when stillness has turned to deafness and
you don't care.

Another quietness is that of deep falling snow. That may be difficult to recall in August. But you can remember, can't you, when
the traffic has all but halted, and sounds are muffled by the soft fluff
of infinite snowflakes.

There is a third quietness. This is the stillness when we are aware
that we are in the presence of God. This is the time when the awesome magnitude of reality is experienced in a deep stillness. It is as
if the noise of a waterfall has been turned off, but its might continues
to roll and tumble.

A waterfall with the sound turned off. Sometimes I think that is
what God is like. The power, foam, strength, and beauty are there.
It is all there. Its power is not in its noise or its roar, but in its ever-
present might.

Experiencing God is like coming upon a giant waterfall with the
sound turned off. It isn't what you would expect, yet, how strong
and real it is. God is at work in decisions, defeats, and victories.

Now and then we catch a glimpse of God as God is, relentlessly
at work, moving, changing, reshaping, fulfilling, and forming the
direction of the stream whose course was set by His doing. But

don't expect a celestial announcement of His Presence. God isn't a waterfall. God is God. But that terrible might and beauty moves on in sturdy silence.

In a world of the unexpected, it is a time for those who sense more than noise and disruption. It is a time for seeking the sturdy quietness of God's mighty stream of intention and way through to quiet waters of determination and purpose. Whatever else we do as a society, let us listen and see the power of the Creator. The breakthroughs needed are ideological, theological, and moral. We can never be moral for others; but in awareness of God, we can strengthen our own morality.

A Lesson on Mutual Respect from a Cat Named Shad

The fact that pets may not like to hear someone whistle, sing, or hum is not unusual. We have a cat named Shad. Upon hearing any of these manifestations of sound, Shad comes, jumps on one's lap, and puts his nose in your face seemingly to beg that the sound cease.

He is not obnoxious about it. In fact, there is a gentleness about the protest that is disarming. Often he will wander into the room, meow, and rub against my legs. If that doesn't put a stop to it, he will jump on my lap in the most affectionate way, put his face against mine, and ultimately break up the melodious output.

It is a rather nice way to protest. At least he is not mean. Actually, one is almost flattered by the style. He may be saying, "I like you, but what you are doing is offensive to my ears." Or, he may be suggesting that we are going to disagree about something that is taking place, but we are going to be friends about it. The relationship is going to stay intact.

As I understand it, he is calling for mutual respect, but there are some things he just can't stand. There is something that keeps Shad and me together.

In any case, I like his style. He isn't threatening to put a shell across my bow, or withdraw his membership in the household, skuttle or limit my activity by actions of aggression or mistrust. He doesn't withhold his confidence in the rights of either of us.

I've been thinking about this as it regards church work, Annual Conference sessions, and international relations. Our cat has a way of giving input into the climate in which action occurs. He is not interested in setting a structure or agenda that modifies our goals or effectiveness. He does not want to scar our relationship. His word seems to be, "Do what you are doing, but take into account that the way you are doing it includes a factor or two that perhaps can be omitted so both of us can function."

Not a bad attitude for the way we do church work or even international relations. Don't break the relationship or the trust level. Just modify the technique. Maybe there is a place in the world for the likes of Shad in human form. It beats tearing a leg off by a long way.

New Year Brings Change

It is snowing today. I was supposed to go to Dallas for a committee meeting that for once was set to take into account my calendar. On awakening this morning, snow was falling and the forecast was for "more and worse." Since I was not to return to Kansas City until late, I could imagine what the drive home from Kansas City might have been like. So I canceled my trip. As far as I know the meeting commenced that had been set by my calendar.

What had been considered by me as a "must" wasn't that after all. It was important but not imperative.

Such is the nature of change. Some change we can design. Some change is designed for us by forces beyond us.

The rub comes in determining whether we use change or are pushed to make change serve us. Given the appropriate attitude we may choose to insist that change will be shaped and formed so as to give evidence of creativity.

This is always a challenge. Since we are up against a new year, it is a time to decide some things. What is God calling us to do? What is God calling us out of? What shall we do with the fresh dose of Christmas spirit? How will it make a difference?

Even at the Kansas East office we are facing change. The main entrance to the building is now at the north door. A receptionist and comfortable chairs are present to personalize an area which for some time has been a work area while the south door has been the entrance to all offices.

Now we have two entrances. To see the conference council or treasurer, we are encouraging the use of the north door. For personnel matters, we are encouraging the use of the previous "main" door, which now exists to welcome persons to the bishop's office and to the Topeka district superintendent's office.

Due to personnel changes brought on by the retirement of key office staff, things will not be as they were.

What a difference is made by a change of familiar faces. What a difference a change of place makes. What does it mean? Well, it can mean what we want it to mean. But meaning occurs best when a feeling of community bridges the past and the future. When relationships have been a blessing, new meaning awaits us if we are "one in the spirit."

Sometimes it is evident that, even in the church, brokenness has a way of causing separation. Much of this brokenness is because we get out of touch. We can mourn for the past or, on the other hand, we can rejoice that our faith provides a unity—a bridge linked by the Unseen which is not a stranger, but is known.

This is family. This is community. This is covenant. Yes, this is really the church. The body of Christ, the New Year, our personal life— all may have several doors, new experiences and encounters. We are bonded by whose we are as well as who we are. We differ, yet remain a network that extends beyond each of us.

I went for a walk in the country near where we live. Several dogs belonging to neighbors went along. One of the dogs got distracted and was left behind to his own interests. I turned around to see if he might be coming and, sure enough, about a fourth of a mile back, there he was, tired but trotting toward us.

I decided to keep going, but one of the dogs saw the laggard and sat down in the road to wait for the other. Then, they came on together to catch up with the rest of the crowd.

No one should be left out or behind in the midst of change. Each

goes at a separate pace. It's all right though, if we keep an eye out
for each other. Somebody gets left behind. Maybe that person gave
time to see something we missed.

The main thing is that we stay connected. We are humans
together. Christians together, children of God together. If you leave
off the word "together," the preceding sentence is essentially without
meaning. Happy New Year!

Learning from Geese in Flight

Riding across Kansas these early mornings, I have noticed numerous formations of geese heading north. A lot has been written about
the formations of these marvelous creatures. Experts believe there
are factors of community, leadership, and care for each other that
enter into this immigration pattern. I suspect there is intelligence as
well as instinct applied in order to make the journey possible.

Whatever the mix of fact and fancy, I hold that a formation of
migrating geese grace the sky with an added dimension of mystery
and beauty. There is order and a design there that holds meaning
and which adds a jewel to the marvel of creation. I don't understand
it, but I experience it as a gift of grace.

What of our migration in and out of society with its seasons of
work, family, joys, and sorrows? Isn't it possible that God intends
the people of God to move with order and intention, acting on the
best of our instincts and intelligence?

If we were in tune with our Creator in a similar fashion, it draws
me to the notion that the church should add grace to the space
through which we move. Many times the congregation of God
loses the rhythm of God's intention. We become distracted, even
embattled with one another.

Pick up today's newspaper and, on a scale of one to ten with ten
being the highest, rate the performance of the world on the quality
of its flight toward God's destiny. You might want to do the same
thing with the announcements in your church bulletin. Matthew
6:10 can give direction to our journey if read seriously: "Thy will
be done on earth as it is in heaven."

Glimpse Christ the Hawk

On these winter days in Kansas, driving has its pleasures including pieces of reverie and reflection. The trees are stark. The prairie is brown. Frequently, one will see a hawk sitting on emaciated tree branches or a fence post.

Now and then, if one looks intently, it is obvious that the head is tilted slightly toward the surrounding earth. A swooping motion is observed at times. Recently, the diving action reverted heavenward and a field mouse or some other small creature was captured. Nature had portrayed and unveiled its drama.

Life is not just a matter of watching the traffic pass. There are forces at work: forces of creation, sometimes of God, sometimes of humans. These, too, interrupt the routine of living out the day.

Here is the question: Is there some linkage that offsets and counter-balances the searching eyes of life? I choose to think there is. God is looking for us, not to destroy and consume but to redeem from chaos to a higher form.

There is a higher sight than that demonstrated in the encounter of hawks and field mice. A God who abides in barren places seeks in order to save, finds in order to redeem, joins in order to give strength and purpose.

If the eyes of the hawk use their cunning, instinctive gift to cap-ture, does not the Creator of the hawk cast eyes of another sort about to seek the lost? There is evidence of Christ the Hawk with the nature of God looking for you and me for a new order that transforms fear into courage, hatred into love, and war into peace.

Will Christ the Hawk find us in time? If we are found by that which claims us to be more than survivors of death, the promise is that we are carried to Life—real Life!

The Hawk that matters is not in a scraggly tree, but in a manger, a child, a decision to be more than we are. The eyes that claim us may be about to penetrate a group, a congregation, or a conference.

The next time I ride across Kansas on a cold day, I think I shall try to catch a glimpse of Christ the Hawk. Maybe He is perched in my mind. He may be harder to see than the one in a lonely Flint

Hills tree. I, the mouse, may not be destroyed but rescued, and I didn't even know I was in the view of his eye. Perhaps it is not the lot of human creatures to find Him, but to be found by Him.

Oh yes, I found myself driving ten miles under the speed limit.

Winter Reluctantly Yields Way to Spring

Have you noticed how much beauty spring has given us whether we deserve it or not? It began, in my case, as the full moon of early March hid its face while awaiting another cycle. In so doing, a glimpse of resurrection peeked like a bright eye from behind winter's curtain. Then there was the haunting sight of occasional migrations of geese winging their journey northward.

I thought, "What grace is our gift as we observe seasons in their annual struggle." Winter is reluctantly letting go while spring attempts to seize the advancing year.

It resembles a babe struggling to be born. In the meantime, we feel both chill and warmth heaving in and out in rhythmic thrusts. If we ever doubt the biblical resurrection accounts, surely nature should lay the issue at rest. New designs and revelations of beauty emerge as virgin birth establishes its own credentials subtly shaped by a Creator whose name is MYSTERY.

A Revelation from Reverie

Once upon a time there was a boy who lived on a farm. His family in that household included mother, father, and grandfather. Circumstances were meager, for those were the dry depression years. But the farm and the home contained warmth and security.

There were times, though, when the isolation of the countryside and being an only child allowed imaginary worlds to take shape. The iron seat of a cultivator sitting unused under a tree could be the saddle of a cowboy hero whose counterpart adventures were shared with goosepimple excitement in the ten-cent Saturday afternoon movie. Driving a team and stalkcutter on a winter afternoon easily became a chariot streaking across the Egyptian desert. The dark

woods enshrouding the riverbank became an African jungle and
the boy was easily another Clyde Beatty, whose escapades in the
deep wilds transported the lad into places far, far away. A rope tied
to a limb overhanging the creek in the wooded pasture became
Tarzan's main street, easily shared in limitless imaginings. First experiences carrying a .22 Remington single-shot rifle on rabbit-hunt-
ing expeditions with Grandfather turned the little rifle into an
elephant gun, since it was just as easy to look for elephants as rabbits
anyway.

As manhood overtook him, nostalgic memories comforted him.
Then, one day—or maybe it was at night in front of the fireplace—
he remembered a fall from a pecan tree when he and his mother
were gathering pecans in the woods. A rotten limb broke and there
was a recollection of the days in bed with a sore tailbone from the
fall. He remembered it well now, though it had long been unrecalled.
The hay mow, which contained caves and private places, had become
a place of fright one day when hay piled high came down, encasing
him in darkness and panic. There were bee stings, sunburns, dog bites,
the death of this own dog by the kick of a horse, the injury of a hen
by a rock thrown that he knew would miss, but didn't.

There was the day when the family's favorite and much-loved
work horse of twenty-one years was shot because the family had to
sell out, and his father couldn't bear to risk someone buying old
Dan who would mistreat him. Dan had been too faithful and too
loved.

And then the boy knew, though now a man, that love, warm
places, dreams, and good times have their opposites. There is no
adventure without risk; no dreams without reality; no laughter without tears; no love without sadness; no high places reached without
occasional falls; no illusions without things as they are.

In quiet revelation, he knew—this boy who had become a
man—that he was now more so a man. I've seen churches like that.
Haven't you?

People Are People Wherever You Go

This summer I have had the opportunity to observe first-hand that our nation possesses geographically a beauty that is astounding. I had occasion to drive my daughter's Jeep a thousand miles to western Nebraska. Even pulling a rental trailer with some of her goods as she completes a move provided a special opportunity to observe the heartland of our Plains state. Then a trip to Vermont, entailing the long 1,700 miles past some of the great cities of America, a train ride to Montreal, a plane trip to a meeting in New York over the hills of New England and back home again elicits a definite feeling of awe and size, but also of appreciation of what we have.

People are people wherever you go. By and large they relate to others who are interested in them. The struggles are the kind that human beings have in common. The enterprise called "human experience" is something approaching the sacred.

And yet, when we turned off Cantrell Road onto Allsopp Park Road on our approach to the house on South Lookout, it was the most beautiful of all. Elaine and I both knew there were problems awaiting us; but also people we know and love. Arkansas is a great state. We just need to look at the hills more, and let our eyes roam the rich vastness of the Delta. Then, to know, if we will, that we are part of the world and a church in the throes of finding our larger identity.

We are part of the community of the world and of the family of humanity. Our politics, our church life, and our personal concerns can never again be narrow and small. We are related to one another. It is a time for unity rather than division, love rather than hate, and peace rather than war. Our well-being will never be secure until the well-being of all humanity is our agenda. How well Jesus knew this. What a price He paid for it.

Changing a Lifestyle

"Your test statistics show that, overall, you are not as old as you really are, except for one thing. You reek of stress and fatigue. Change your lifestyle or we will be calling on you in a nursing home. You are a wall socket with too many appliances plugged in. Cancel what you have on your schedule for a month."

Well, my attention was gained. It took nearly a month to get out of things I was scheduled to be into. But, after the funeral of Bishop Shamblin in Baton Rouge, Elaine and I headed for New England. I thought we would never get there (which was a symptom that had to be shed). We spent a week on the Maine coast. I hiked the beaches, sat on the massive rocky shore while the surf pounded and sprayed, strolled daily through a little artistic fishing town, watched the lobster boats come in, and took lots of pictures.

We drove up through New Hampshire, still taking pictures of the leaves and taking our time. At one point it seemed to me that the counter on the camera was indicating a full roll of film had been used, but when I opened the camera, there was no film in it. Elaine lost two nights' sleep laughing at the look on my face.

The trip was pleasantly uneventful except for nice experiences— mostly. We stopped at a motel in Vermont. The units were rather compact and identical. After we got settled, I went to the office to get a paper, came back, entered the room, and noticed that the TV was on a different channel. Elaine wasn't around. I sat down to watch. There was a knock on the door. I answered the knock and greeted two elderly ladies standing there who informed me I was in their room. Embarrassed, I apologized and went to our room. Elaine lost another night's sleep laughing.

Placing some real film in my camera, we stopped alongside a beautiful lake with surrounding hills covered with beautiful foliage. I stopped the car, very carefully took a couple of pictures, carefully put the lens cover back on, and promptly got into the back seat looking for the steering wheel. As usual, it was up front. I was misplaced again. That didn't help Elaine's sleep that night, either.

A few days in Burlington, Vermont, in the home of some friends who live in Fort Smith, were heaped with rest and interesting things. A family matter with relatives in Nashville brought the New England stay to a close, and we headed toward home, caring for our

errand on the way. But Allsopp Park Road leading to our house
was a welcome sight. Refreshed we were, and thankful to God for
journeying mercies. I've had the lectures on changing lifestyles. I
can recite them. Practicing them is a bit harder. I guess that's the
way it is with the Christian faith. Life is a journey in faith. There is
more than we know and do. Anyway, I know that God is in the
coming and going of the tide. The breakers are still pounding the
coastline as they have for millions of years. There is a tide, though,
that is always at our feet and its name is God.

The pictures that we didn't take are in our minds. In fact, my
mind has translated those absent pictures into movies. At night when
I go to bed, I still feel and see the heavy surf in glorious movement.
I walk the beaches after the tide has receded and search the debris
wondering where the pieces of rope came from, who belonged to
the pair of good shoes entwined with seaweed. Were they washed
overboard? Was the man they belonged to washed overboard? I bask
in the quiet splendor of beautiful fall trees challenging rays of sun
in special ways. I almost wonder why I bothered to try to take pictures. Perhaps, though, it was good that I focused through the film-
less lens so as to see things in particular and not just in general. A
particular tree, a special wave, a human being rather than humanity—maybe I need to focus more carefully to see the beautiful and
holy. After all, Moses saw God in a particular bush. Which person,
which place is the space where God is trying to reveal himself? I
must look more carefully.

What Is Your Burning Bush?

In the third chapter of Exodus the story is told abut a day when
Moses was taking care of the sheep and goats of his father-in-law,
Jethro. In the course of his duties, he saw a bush on fire. What follows
is an account describing how his inquiry about the bush caused him
to confront not just a burning bush, but the voice of God coming
from the bush.

Now Moses was no mere visionary. Earlier, perhaps out of a mix
of compassion and vengeance, he had killed a man whom he saw

murder a Hebrew man. So, Moses, like us, had in him the best and worst impulses of most humans.

Anyhow, the experience with the bush afire turned into an encounter with the reality of God that made even the ground on which Moses was standing assume the nature of holy ground. Wherever we are aware of God's presence and claim on us, it is a holy place and a holy moment.

It was a costly encounter for Moses, however, because God told him that he, Moses, must become involved in the mistreatment of His people in Egypt and lead them out of the country. That's troubling. It is always troubling as well as comforting to have a religious experience. The Lord usually has something for us to do that sometimes scares the rags off us.

This leads me to suggest that a burning bush is really not so much a place. It is a moment of insight when the inventory of life confronts us. A burning bush is a fresh awareness that we cannot run away. Even such an unsuspecting incident as a burning bush, an unsuspecting unchurched moment in life, may hold sacred content—even God.

When we come to such a moment, we say "yes" or "no" to its claim. A burning bush may be an experience of surrender. It is a feeling of reassurance that we are not our own. It is a piece of time in which we are called to engage what God mandates to be changed.

A burning bush is a moment of truth when the experience of the holy and divine is so overwhelming that it obviously calls for response. It seemed to Moses that God was saying something like, "There are people in Egypt, Moses, who are enslaved and entrapped in circumstances that are not decent. You are to lead them out of that situation into a new future."

It is obvious that a burning bush, then, is a time when risk must be engaged. It is a point when we stop enduring history and determine to seize it in order to give it new form.

Moses' experience suggests to me that a burning bush confronts us in United Methodism, as well as being in an occasional personal experience. Are we aware that God is among us? How will we respond? What say you to the idea that we form a Burning Bush Society? There is room in the society for all who will respond.

CHAPTER
2

Lessons to Be Learned

God's People

We must walk where He walks, or He does not walk.
We must be in the place He wants us to be,
    or His presence will not be known.
We must decide where He decides, or the decision is not His.
We must stand where He would stand, or He does not stand.
We must speak where He would speak, or He is not heard.
We must weep where He would weep, or there is no caring.

There is a presence where He is,
    and our presence will give substance to
    what might seem to be His absence.
My hope gives voice to His silence,
    for in His distance He is near.
In His silence He is able to speak.
He who is not visible is real,
    if I allow Him to occupy who and what I am.
        KWH

A Growing Faith

Genesis brings to us a growing faith because it tells us of our beginnings. Humanity—all humanity—came from God. This truth has been troublesome to some. A generation or two ago the monkey theory was bounced around vigorously. Facetiously, maybe we had that theory turned around when we talked about man descending from monkeys. I haven't heard anyone, scientist or otherwise, saying that monkeys are becoming more like people but we see people acting like monkeys all the time.

Then there are those who, believing in the development of the human through the centuries of primitive manners, declare that such thorough-going evolution refutes the book of Genesis, making it obsolete, untrue, thus necessitating the scrapping of a religious faith founded upon the Bible. Another group refutes the evidence that science has accumulated and steadfastly clings to a literal reading of the Genesis accounts.

What persons in all these categories are doing is what a person of 150 years ago might do if he came upon someone putting gasoline into the tank of a car. He might say, "Why, pouring a bucket of watery-looking fluid into a tank fastened onto a large arrangement of heavy metal can't possibly make that contraption move at the high speed you claim." That person would not be understanding the nature of the fluid going into the tank nor the nature of the contraption itself. So with the details regarding human beginnings as recorded in Genesis. Neither the skeptic nor the literalist is understanding the nature of that beginning, or the nature of the author's design written into that literature.

A person—probably several persons—centuries ago were desiring to give an account of the origin of man that could be told around the campfires, in the tents while the dark hours of the late evening were passing. It was to be a story that one generation could pass on to the other; a story that would contribute to the religious life of a people. It was told in a way that would endure. It was meant to be a vehicle of faith that would provide growth to the hearts of a people when they were in famine, in war, in tribulation. They should always remember that they came from God. The fish of the sea, the birds of the air, the animals of the field, and human beings—all had common beginning. They came from God.

So we have the ape theory or the dust theory—and neither has anything to brag about until we get at the heart of the matter. We must learn that the greatest truth this side of Jesus is ("In the beginning, God . . . ," and "God created man in his own image") God's imagination. God used his own imagination in the creation of this creature, and that creature bore the marks of being a living soul.

That tells you whether the world is worth saving or not. That tells us whether or not there is dignity in being a human. There in that drama of Genesis the worth of life takes a design. In Genesis, we find a basis for a growing faith because it tells us of our Divine beginnings.

This story (Genesis 3) further contributes to the growing faith of the ages by showing us the nature of humanity without God. For one thing, look at their reaction when confronted by their own sin. God said, "Have you eaten of the tree which I commanded you not to eat?" The man said, "The woman whom you gavest to be with me, she gave me fruit of the tree and I ate." Perhaps I hear a wife saying, "Isn't that just like a man—always blaming his wife for something he did wrong. Adam couldn't even be a first-class sinner." But wait till you hear Eve's excuse. "Then the Lord God said to the woman, 'What is this that you have done?' The woman said, 'The serpent beguiled me and I ate.'" Neither one accepted the consequences of their actions.

Traditionally we have said that the serpent is the counterpart of Satan. But isn't it just like people, when they can't blame their mischief on anyone else, to blame it on the Devil? Adam blamed Eve and Eve blamed the serpent. What we have here is an excellent portrayal of the psychology of sin. Never blame yourself. Blame your parents, your childhood environment, your wife, but never yourself. "My teacher gave me a complex as a child." "My parents made me attend church when I was young. That's why I don't go now." That was Adam's way of getting out of it. The writer of Genesis is saying that it is human rationale for sinful action. Eve took a more religious approach. She blamed the serpent (Satan?) for her foolishness. *But the truth of Genesis is that, in the sight of God, both are responsible!* The truth of this portion of God's word is serious truth.

Adam and Eve were never as real back there in a garden as they are right here. It was intended to be so, for we are speaking here of a faith that has grown through the centuries. The consequences of their choice between good and evil are our consequences, too. Their way of standing up to the judgment of God is our way; and God's way of confronting them is still God's way. God still says of human behavior today, "What is this that you have done?" We still have to answer to the same moral judgment for our personal and our corporate behavior.

The Genesis story continues. The writer relates the account of all the world under the judgment of a God who will not condone evil. The story of one faithful man named Noah is told about how Noah became an instrument of God's righteousness. The writer connects his own kindred to Noah through the lineage of Noah, and Abram emerges to father a people that would be God's people.

Yes, a garden was the setting for the drama of humanity's humble beginning. In a garden, humanity learned the consequences of sin. In their garden experience they learned that God was there. The future dimensions of humanity's self-development were set forth in that garden. It was in a garden that another person learned the consequences of human sin. In the first garden, the first man was called to bear the guilt of his sin. In the Garden of Gethsemane, a man was called upon to bear the guilt of all sin.

In Gethsemane, Jesus' idea of God was at stake. Is the human being truly a moral being? Is God a God of love? Is right stronger than wrong? Is love stronger than hate? Can humanity refute the righteousness of God and escape the penalty? Will God forsake one who is completely submerged in His will and His spirit of love? Can the light that God gave the world in Jesus be quenched? As the hymn says, "Jesus paid it all" to find out.

The first man tried to discover how little of God was in the garden. Jesus tried to discover how much of God was in the garden. Adam shows the destiny of a human who tries to escape God. Jesus shows the destiny of a human who tries to submerge himself in God's will and spirit.

There will be Gethsemanes and crosses, but the outcome is clear. There is Easter. The outcome can be ours. We need only acknowledge the wonder as well as the reality of God. The first garden shows us our human beginnings. In the second, we have our destiny. In the garden of sin and guilt, God was there. In the garden of trial and dedication, God is there.

Whatever may be the garden of our experience, God is always there and always ready to bring resurrection to crucified years, crucified hopes. The life of Jesus as the object of our dedication will set the Adam in all of us free and eternal to till the ground of God's purpose forever.

Conversion to Servanthood Evangelism

There is something troublesome about being old enough to have been a contemporary of Hiroshima, Nagasaki, Auschwitz, Vietnam, Selma, the Iranian hostage incident, the prison crisis, pornography peddlers, alcohol and drug abuse to the extent that these have commanded the attention of our society. There are signs which suggest that we are on the verge of succumbing both to numbness and rage. These are real ingredients in my life, my world and God's. These along with some positive achievements, thankfully, are the world in which my spiritual journey and my ministry must take place.

I have to believe a person is bluffing who might say, "I'm not a part of this because I am a Christian." Yet, I know that the impact of unsavory human experiences are bound to elicit varied ways of responding to the realities of life.

As one whose life is pretty nearly absorbed in the dynamics of values as set forth by the Christian Gospel, there is continuous deciding as a Christian minister and as a bishop relative to what being a responsible follower of Christ means.

As a pastor I have seen many people die. A pastor over a lifetime of ministry will have had dozens of occasions of being with those who experience the solitude and the rage of the heart's desert when life has turned parched and unproductive. A pastor of people will have been asked to lead persons out of bondage to horizons of hope over and over again.

So what does being a follower of the Christian Way mean? Does one try to change the desert, or on the other hand, does one content oneself with making people satisfied with it in the knowledge that someday we will die and be taken from it?

A study of the Gospels will surprise the reader as one discovers that in the presence of death, Jesus, time and time again, is described as having compassion on the people in the situation. A hurried look in a concordance will reveal "compassion" as a word used repeatedly in describing Jesus' response to death, hunger, and loneliness. This feature in His character is so dominant that it becomes a mark of style in His ministry.

I think the church and its people are short on compassion and long on judgment. The answer is too simplistic, I know, but I'll state it anyway. I believe we have short circuited the salvation act by stopping with the central dimension of Christian discipleship, that of conversion. Make no mistake about it, conversion is central, basic, essential, and at the core of salvation! I say this lest I be accused of not believing in conversion. Conversion is what the ministry of the church is all about.

But then Jesus says to me, "Follow me," and there is talk about a cup of cold water, visitation in prison, and being provided clothing when naked—all in His name. There is also talk about taking up our cross and following Him. This is the lifestyle of those who would believe that Jesus meant it when He said, "I have come that they might have life and have it abundantly."

From this point of view, conversion is the stance that turns us toward servanthood in the world in which and for which Christ gave His life. I am asked in varied ways, as are most ministers, to stop with a concern for salvation or to be content with saving souls.

But when is salvation a reality or when is a soul saved? Suppose when one experiences conversion that that individual finds the nerve endings of compassion exposed, and concern for the humanity which is God's manifested? What happens if, as a result of conversion, one senses that the near edge of God is in the un-Christlike ways of our social structure? Then, how does one obey? It may be that at some point the experiencing of Christ is to experience the cup Jesus had in mind when He asked, "Can you drink of the cup of which I drink?"

All of this is to say that conversion without the struggle of finding the meaning of obedience and faithfulness in the issues of peace, justice, poverty, legislation, and human rights is, for some of us, unthinkable. We may not agree as to what God is saying, but not to struggle in the hearing, not to strain in the seeing of His purpose and will would be heresy. I cannot be an evangelical dropout. Evangelism is witness, but evangelism is also servanthood. Christ is at work in too many places and in too many people for Him to be left alone.

The extent to which Jesus is heard and seen in legislative halls, in courtrooms, school board meetings, U.N. meetings, and the like is as important as His being seen and heard in church. What goes on in the so-called secular arena is laden with values and judgments that affect the human situation.

What should be the spirit of the church in dealing with the community side of life? (Here I speak of community globally as well as locally.) My conviction is that the time has arrived in the life of our society and the church when the role of the church is not so much as antagonist or protagonist as it is presenter of the claims of Christ in a pastoral spirit. Much needed is a witness that finds expression through a spirit of caring that emerges out of the strong spiritual interior of God's people.

Our day seems satiated with hardened attitudes, even in the disguise of righteousness that will not tolerate diversity. When an evangelism of servanthood is added to the evangelism of witness, the church runs the risk of rejection and suffering. The servant in Isaiah 53 is thus described. This servant in Isaiah is usually thought of in

Christian circles as descriptive of Jesus. The passage may also describe the model of Jesus' church, the one of which you and I are members.

In any case, it is clear that in Isaiah's time, or in any time, God's Word is alive in history, even in that of which we are a part. This means that Christians must confront the sins of the world, which also means being vulnerable to risk, to mistakes, even failure, but always attempting to minister with compassion.

Dr. Bruce Birch of Wesley Theological Seminary in Washington, D.C., asks a poignant question for all to consider: "Can a church preoccupied with institutional success and burdened by material comfort go to the cross for the sake of wholeness in a broken world?" It appears that some of our lack of certitude contains the struggle toward that decision. Can we link arms and hearts together in love and grace to seek the answer? Unless we do, it does not appear that the answer will be found.

Moral Majority

When it comes to identifying candidates who are of one's own political persuasion, I find the approach used by "Moral Majority" to be about the worst way to do it. Pick an issue, any issue. Find one or more texts in the Bible about that issue, or something close to it, that you believe states your point of view about that issue; or, if you wish, turn it around and form your opinion on the basis of the holy writ you have found. Then go out and find a candidate who is on the same side of that issue as you. The candidate may have no history of Christian commitment or involvement in the mission of the church, but that really doesn't matter. The Moral Majority advocate has found scripture to support his or her issue. He or she has found a candidate to support that issue. The process is moral, so goes the assumption. And for the sake of clout, more of these people gather in crowds and talk louder than the other bunch. So they must be in the majority.

Shame on Christians who stoop to such trivia. It isn't Christian—

it is manipulation, pure and simple. Whether it has to do with relaxing the speed limit, keeping women in their place, showing the Russians who is boss, or praying out loud in school, it's a cool, simple-minded way of hoodwinking ourselves into thinking God is on our side; or, for that matter, of thinking we have, by such chicanery, put ourselves in God's camp.

The procedure doesn't bother to ask what a candidate's overall value orientation is. It doesn't care whether a candidate takes a view because it's popular or because that view holds a long-range advantage for the candidate. It doesn't bother with how the candidate's value system would be expressed on other issues. The candidate can hold the proper view on my favorite issue and be a very ungodly person in terms of honesty and integrity that should be available for other issues.

Another shame in it all is that scripture shows God coming down heavily on matters of justice, poverty, and the imprisoned. There is even special mention made of the blessedness due to those who are peacemakers. Such undeniable evidence in the reality of the scripture seems to be overlooked.

There are many modern issues on which Jesus did speak. There are many on which He did not speak, but I see in the Gospels a style in which Jesus, just by that style, has an authority that places high value on spirituality being a stance, a direction a Christian takes in viewing all of life, all issues. Speaking personally, my "born again" experience has brought me to some convictions that happen to be my stance in faith. I am not always right in my positions, but this is my place. It is where my fundamental faith in the God of Jesus Christ has brought me at this time. The ethics I see being used by "Moral Majority" folk to reflect an oppressive, ruthless, authoritarianism that is willing to destroy any spiritually motivated leaders is a style that for me and my faith is not only unmoral, but unChristian. Where I happen to be in my position reflects my conviction and my place of holy ground, which I believe is viable in view of my understanding of the claims of the Gospel. Whether "Moral

Majority" likes it or not, I, too, find Christ in the conclusions of my own Christian consideration.

From reading the "Moral Majority" positions, they would get everything they want and peace would still be undernourished, the problem of nuclear waste would still be unresolved, the hungry of the world would still be hungry, the thousands of political prisoners in oppressive countries will still be there, the environment continues to be desecrated without regard as to what its limits are in supporting the race, women will still be treated by the law differently than are men. I must know a candidate's view on those issues, for they, too, are moral issues and are the targets of decisions which are made by moral values or the absence of moral values.

I pray that people will vote out of a conscience of values shaped by the Lord of the Bible. II Chronicles has a good word for this moment: "If my people who are called by name humble themselves, and pray and seek my face, and turn from their wicked ways, then I will hear from heaven, and forgive their sin and heal their land." This was in the Bible of Jesus. It is a word from one who hears the prayers of Jews and Gentiles alike, or of anyone else who prays in its spirit.

Vote! Vote for candidates who have a spiritual eye to the whole world and to all its people. Vote for persons whom you believe have a passion to reflect, as best they can, the calm conscience of the Almighty in All issues, who are able to see God's creation and all His children as those for whom He gives himself.

God Suffers with Us

The tragedy of Steve Little, former kicker for the Arkansas Razorbacks and for the St. Louis Cardinals, is a matter to ponder. Steve experienced the pressure of being put to the test regarding his skills, then was dismissed because he was not "productive" enough.

Following some "down" hours, which were also "unproductive" but understandable, he was in a car accident last week and is not expected to be able to walk again. We pray the diagnosis is wrong.

Steve provided Razorback fans with thrilling, almost unbelievable, field goals. He was the first-round draft choice for a pro-football kicker.

Since his accident, it is reported that Steve said, "It is God's will." I hope the message gets to Steve that it was not God's will. God isn't that kind of God.

I don't know why the pieces of life went together as they did to form the fragile potential that resulted in the tragic fragmenting of dreams. But God's will? I think not. God does not will in a vacuum of decency and humaneness. God is more merciful, not less, than we are. We are not set up by divine intervention for disaster. God wants goodness, not badness.

One is driven to say, "But, it isn't fair." And there we all have to agree, including God. Nowhere, though, are we promised that life is fair. That's not the promise. The promise is that we are not alone. This was the discovery of Jesus. "Why hast thou forsaken me?" was replaced by assurance that God was in the event.

All of us are fragile vessels that are weaker than the blows that life sometimes issues us. We may, or may not, experience those blows that shatter and devastate; but no one is guaranteed immunity. The Bible is full of that which is unfair. Closer to home, we are saddened by personal examples we could name.

The fragile vessel of clay that is our life was made by a potter who designed us in the image of love, grace, and presence. That is the portion that is not destroyed. That reality is with us, not to answer our questions, but to keep us from being alone.

The triumph is not being free from misfortune, but in being free from bitterness. The glory is not in having our fragility untouched, but in having our brokenness blessed with that love which never leaves us, never lets us go. The victory is not in our unbrokenness, but in the promise that "Thou art with me." This is the ultimate test of us—and of God. But the cross and the empty tomb is our promise that He never discontinues His relationship with us. He is never beyond us. Instead, He is as close as breath itself. He is in the suffering so intimately that He suffers, too, and that gives life its meaning.

We Can Provide Food for the World's Population

I must say that I am proud of the initiative United Methodists have taken regarding the day of the Interfaith Hunger Ingathering bringing together that which will sustain life for human beings who do not have it so good. Our church in Arkansas has germinated a thousand flowers of beautiful stewardship.

People continue to be hungry around the world. But a turn in events is taking place. In the midst of an era of persistent hunger and poverty, this fertile earth produces more than enough food to meet our needs today. This news comes from a recent publication of *The Hunger Project* published in San Francisco.

Then why are people hungry? The answer lies in such areas as poverty, politics, imperfect distribution systems, and faulty motivation. Basically, people who have money have food. People who do not have money are short of food.

But the good news is that we can provide food for the world's population. It is up to people to express their influence. The action required is largely from governments, but it is people who can create the understanding and awareness that requires our systems to act.

There is a spiritual dimension to the physical problems of hunger. In John 6 Jesus said, "Do not labor for the food which perishes, but for the food which endures to eternal life." The people said to Him, "Lord, give us this bread always." Jesus said to them, "I am the bread of life; he who comes to me shall not hunger."

We who are Christians believe that in this truth lies our motivation to respond. The hunger of the world will be met as human spirits are fed with the direction and nature of Jesus Christ. The changes resulting are personal, but the hardest ones are the corporate changes. We must translate our personal fullness into decisions that enable that fullness to be experienced by people everywhere.

This New Week . . .

Today is Monday so who can tell
If the week will be one of heaven or hell.
I'll do my best and give my all.
When challenge comes, I'll take the call.
But, Lord, there are problems from the past week,
The answers for which I continue to seek.
The week is new but the agenda's old.
I need to be vigorous; I need to be bold.
Grant me courage to bow my neck
And refuse to be a nervous wreck.
Life holds your Presence and is filled with Grace.
It's much better than what's in second place.

KWH

The Missing Ingredient

Sometimes the thought saturates my mind that a missing ingredient in our church life is that of righteous indignation. In recent days, I have noted several articles in newspapers and magazines telling of the frightening desecration of our oceans and rivers.

Jeremy Rifkin, prominent critic and student of the social and environmental scene, says that we can now boast of killing off one of God's creatures every sixty minutes. During the course of the next twelve years, says Rifkin, we will have exterminated nearly 20 percent of the remaining species left on the planet.

Then there are the documented incidents of dishonesty in defense contracts. Laws set by Congress are flagrantly defied within the government itself. Tests on defense weapons have been adjusted to give us equipment that does not work.

My point in describing these things is to further say that surrounding this reality is an appalling complacency. The predicament appears to have been accompanied by a numbness as if this is the way life has to be. One would think that people of conscience would be enraged.

My next annoying thought is that there seems to be a spillover that is observed in the notion that God's people surely would be compelled to express indignation and perhaps even rage.

The vibrancy of our church is not all that it should or can be. God must grieve at the degree to which all of us, lay and clergy together, give silent consent to things as they are.

The corruption and marginal morality evident in our social systems has immunized us to the spiritual disorder in our Christian witness, or so it would seem. What shall we say then to these things?

Last year our two conferences experienced a loss of membership just short of 4,000. I have looked for signs of faithfulness that some remote way might indicate other Christian actions which might have taken temporary priority over a concern for lost members.

The evidence is lacking. We have been tamed by our culture; thus our proclamation and mission as a church has been deprived of Christian passion.

I hasten to add that many good things are occurring in many congregations. But I am writing out of the view looming at large which presents itself. If new things are not happening in the lives of our people, why is such the case?

Most of the needed corrections do not require new conference programs or added budgets. We have the personal freedom to move deeper into God. We can meet around scripture, engage in prayer, and design our message to reflect caring and hope.

New hope and a new day are getting great press from the politicians. Can that message that is uniquely the Christian message find channels of expression in and through us? Is this not a day for "holy rage" to be couched in the transforming message of the risen Christ?

I believe that bold witnessing and obedience must become us. We must see the church at work in obedience. That tells the world that a new thing has come to pass. Christ is alive! The world and all that is in it is God's. We must respond together. The Christ and His message are ours to give away. As the old hymn says, "Why Not Now?"

Hurt By What We Do Not Know

What you don't know can hurt you. This past week, while renewing her driver's license, Elaine decided to inquire from the tax collector authorities as to the status of our house taxes. We haven't had a notice of taxes due for a long time. She discovered that our house taxes were delinquent for at least two years and was informed by the clerk that for $1,800 someone could have had possession of our house. The news was so disconcerting that surely there must be some explanation as to why we aren't even on the mailing list to say nothing of why a delinquent notice was not sent. The only answer was, "That's not the way it's done." The hour was late in the day, so adequate protest or clarification was not possible evidently.

But, you know something? We are going to find out the reasons. The last receipt we have was stamped "paid" on the wrong side, so, according to the clerk, it cannot be honored; thus collection was made for those taxes as well.

Something is wrong with the system. Something is wrong with a lot of systems.

To top it all off, they didn't want to take anything but cash, and my good wife wasn't about to trust such a system with cash. Reluctantly the check was accepted, but no receipt could be given for it.

The point in airing this Hicks household linen is to say, "What you don't know can hurt you." Who else has been hurt, perhaps irreparably, by what they didn't know? Whose homes have been quietly snookered?

In another vein, whose minds have gone undeveloped because of the lack of opportunity to learn? How many lives will be deprived of being prepared for usefulness because schools such as Philander Smith will not be able to offer higher education to students due to the progressing pinch on funds that provide college education to needy students. How many will not be able to go to Hendrix because of the absence of student loan funds?

Or for another side to the "knowing" coin, for how many people is hope withheld because they do not know that God cares and that His presence sustains and upholds. Then, there are those who are the victims of history, culture, sex, color, or exploitation of various kinds.

The Christian message is a message to persons, and to systems as well. We are responsible for each other, or it appears we had better be, or the systems become our masters instead of our servants.

Methinks the doctrine of salvation falls short until we who are Christian take it seriously enough to include justice in our Gospel and in our daily decisions. All of God's children need love, grace, shoes, and bread.

Heroes or Witnesses

It is appropriate to have models who inspire us and move us toward right behavior. There is a difference, however, between heroes who are celebrities to be admired and heroes whose witness reveals a deep current of faith whose source is God.

Paul and Barnabas were instrumental in the healing of a man in Lystra. The outcome was that the people were so fascinated by the spectacular aspects of the act they could or did not appreciate the deeper, more sacred dimensions of the event. They tried to make celebrities of Paul and Barnabas.

To those of us who have the advantage of the elapsed years of appreciation for the impact of these Christian servants, we can rightly say that they are heroes of the Christian faith. The reason such appraisal is valid likely stems from the fact that Paul and Barnabas proclaimed a deeper reality of the healing event. They reminded the crowd that they were human. Their admonition affirmed that their humanity was related to God "who made the heaven and the earth and the sea and all that is in them."

Paul and Barnabas saw their actions as a witness to God. God, to them, was no magician. God is God. Paul and Barnabas were two human beings whose lives were dedicated to the manifestation of God's love and care for others.

It is correct to use the term *heroes* for Paul and Barnabas in the sense that they allowed their humanness to be used by God. They dispelled the idea proposed by their admirers that the beginning and end of their powers were in themselves.

As God and divine law move the currents and tides of the sea in keeping with the intention of creation, there is a sense in which that same creative law provides the currents on which the actions of faithfulness flow in and out of the sea of human experience. Our lives can bear witness to that. When we know it and do it, all relationships are given quality.

Paul and Barnabas felt the pull of God. The crowd felt the pull of sensationalism. The best heroes are the heroes of God who know their humanness. Thank God for it, and allow its blessing to make use of what we are and what we can do for others.

The greatest heroes are those whose humanity is likened to God and whose lives move in rhythm to the deeper movement of God's intentions. Out of such awareness comes healing and creation.

Hunger Walk

The walk for hunger was today.
The aching muscles, the blisters were
        in full array.
But we walked because they walk.
They walk farther than we did
        to reach a doctor.
The suffering of the world
Will little benefit from our steps
And from the few thousand dollars we raised,
But we saved a life or two for some further
        fulfillment.
It was most worthwhile,
For we walked as they walk.
In fifty-one years I have never walked fifteen miles
        in one day for anything or anybody.
But there are bodies encasing persons
Who walk and suffer daily
Without my food, the love I know or
        the bed that gives rest to a weary body.
Tomorrow, they know aches of body and soul I will
        never know.
My walk is over. Theirs goes on.
I may have helped a bit today.
But most of all I felt a bit of what they feel—
        the hopeless
        the helpless
        the hungry
        the sick.
God, help me walk in their footsteps daily,
        in the footsteps and paths they will never escape.

Lord, let the rice we provide today be accompanied
       by my daily concern.
The walk is over; the compassion must continue.
Let it be so, Lord. Let it be so.

                  KWH

CHAPTER

3

Advent and Christmas

At Christmastime

Violence is in the land,
This land of hope and dreams.
Where has tolerance gone?
When human beings draw guns and knives,
    there is no peace.
Preach peace, speak of freedom to be,
    not "freedom to get."
They want us to speak of the rapture,
    of Satan, of Hell.
I say, "speak of love, understanding, and reconciliation.
Speak of justice."
They would have us preach of that which does not
    matter in language that does not matter;
Of that which contains no risk, changes no laws,
    no lives.
The gospel of escape is not the Gospel of Jesus.
He would not let them escape or avoid
    consideration of the poor and the unlovely.
In so doing, neither did He escape.
But, He verified the side God is on.
God drew near and said, "From this I can make
Resurrection!"

Thus, we go on with the same struggle that killed Him.
In the dilution of His Word in human form,
    Christians may be the ones that are the enemy
        of themselves and of humankind.

Will the baby make it out of the manger this Christmas?
God is not on the side of the narrow, the self-righteous,
    even when they invoke the name, "Christian."

Let us press the babe so closely to our breast
    that He becomes who we are with His kingdom in us.
                KWH

Advent—A Time for Sacred Deeds, Words, and Symbols

Why is it that we often become so tired and exhausted during these days just prior to Christmas. Maybe it is because we try to move into Christmas around December 1 instead of seeing these December days as a time of preparation and expectation. The way many of us handle Advent reminds one of the experience of trying to step off an escalator before one gets to the top. A person gets all shaken up but doesn't make the landing.

I don't know just how to make the transition from where you and I are in our local setting and personal schedule over to the intention of scripture and the church season. But, somebody knew we would try to get ahead of ourselves, thus the season of Advent.

Advent is a time of preparation of self (mind, spirit, faith) so that the arrival of the Christ child can be fully experienced and appreciated.

It isn't intended that we move immediately from Thanksgiving to Christmas. Advent is that in-between time that lies amid what we have experienced and the "not yet, but going to be."

There is something flawed with the process of starting the season with gift planning, gift acquisition, celebration events with yuletide frenzy, as if Christmas is already here. The result is that we are tired when the time for Celebration and Joy does arrive.

Now, I don't know just what to do about this situation. It is like driving a car that is out of time with itself. The engine works against itself.

If we are not to work against ourselves we might give attention to preparing the expectant heart. Let's try to learn to see joy and goodness in one another.

There comes a time when (to use a knife-sharpening term) we must hone the soul so that we can hear sounds of hope in children, see possibilities of the future in the world around us, and be alert to the presence of sacred deeds, words, and symbols.

Technically, I suppose this would mean delaying the purchase of gifts until after Christmas Day. We won't do that. That's too radical. But don't rush into Christmas! Enjoy the season of anticipation.

Advent is YOUR time, when you might hear cheerful songs in unusual places, and take into account the promises and intentions of God for all of us. Then when Christmas arrives we are prepared within to embrace newness, hope, and love as typical of a life that is worth carrying into the season of Light.

No Manger in the Yellow Pages

Just for fun I looked in the Yellow Pages to see if I could find the word "manger." There are classifications of all sorts, none of which has any relationship to the others. The products and services listed, however, constitute what the average person might desire.

Churches and restaurants take a lot of space in the Yellow Pages—but mangers? Apparently a manger is not a hot item. There are machine shops, machine tools, magazine distributors, magician supplies, magnets, maid consultants, manufacturers agents, maps, and marble, but no mangers.

The angels said to the shepherds concerning Jesus, "You will find him wrapped in swaddling clothes lying in a manger." Just suppose those nervous shepherds had said, "Oh, my goodness, let's see who features mangers in Bethlehem." Suppose they had rushed to the nearest phone booth and hurriedly turned to the Yellow Pages. They would have gone down the list mentioned above, but no manger! Isn't the place where the Christ child is dwelling one of the categories in the Yellow Pages? Everything else is pigeonholed so perfectly. Why can't Jesus be that way?

The shepherds looked up, and the glory of God in the Highest led them to Bethlehem. When they arrived they noticed, not a manger, but life's Master. The place where the Christ child lay turned out to be—not in the hay—but in their heart.

There are some things you will find nowhere else except in your heart. Lay the Yellow Pages aside, along with the stock quotations, and the price lists. There is something you are looking for which you won't find anywhere but in your heart.

For us, there is no Bethlehem. There is no star. There is only your heart. You have probably looked everywhere else, but have you looked there? If you did, didn't you find Him?

The message of Christmas is that you and I can find Him; and when we do, we will have found God. The affirmation of the angels was, "Glory to God in the Highest, and on earth . . ." That is the clue—"on earth . . ."

There is no manger, but there are lowly humble places on earth. He is born on earth in the hearts of people. God's glory is our gift.

May that glory be your gift throughout the New Year.

In the Still, Unlikely Presence

It's funny what little nuances of joy enter into a holiday season. There are the big things, of course, which matter most, such as the theological dimensions of Christmas and the ponderings related to what it means to begin again with a new year and the fact that symbolically the new year is God's gift. There were some less profound matters that I thoroughly enjoyed, however. There has been time to sharpen my knife, to shine my shoes, and read the Christmas cards. I even took Elaine out to breakfast one morning in my jeans and flannel shirt. It was fun: eggs, hashbrowns, and biscuits never tasted so good.

I don't expect this description of the holiday time to be appreciated by everyone, but, at our house, there isn't much time for the "small stuff." Still, I wonder which is most important. For a moment or two or three there was a special blessing of time for the un-earth-shaking, noncontroversial personal kind of linkage with a greater reality. An unhurried time for the fireplace, family, and a little reflection may not help United Methodism much, but as to whether it had spiritual content there can be no doubt. It has not been a program, a thrust, a ministry, except that I thought I caught a glimpse of God once or twice that I haven't seen for a while.

If you, dear reader, know what I am talking about, you will know what I mean when I propose that they were right that night in Bethlehem. In the still, unlikely presence of loved ones, friends, animals, and a star of hope, the other issues take on a different dimension. Our passing this way does not matter so much in what we *do* but in what we *are* to each other.

New Design for the Future

> *The wolf shall dwell with the lamb, and the leopard*
> *shall lie down with the kid, and the calf and the lion and*
> *the fatling together, and the little child shall lead them.*
> *The cow and the bear shall feed; their young shall lie*
> *down together; and the lion shall eat straw like the ox.*
> *The suckling child shall play over the hole of the asp, and*
> *the weaned child shall put his hand on the adder's den.*
> *They shall not hurt or destroy in all my holy mountain;*
> *for the earth shall be full of the knowledge of the Lord as*
> *the waters cover the sea.—Isaiah 11:6–9*

What does one do with such an idyllic passage? We can add it to the collection of moving sayings, stories, prophecies, and scenes which bring warmth and appreciation to the deep relationships of life. Such action will certainly enhance the meaning of Advent.

There is another approach, however. There may be some worth gleaned in considering this passage as a radical vision of a new future. The tender images of the wolf and the lamb, the leopard with a young goat, the calf abiding in peace with the lion reach a level of extremity in the declaration that a little child shall lead them.

It would be wise for us to note the verses preceding this passage. We are given a description of the actions of a dynamic, caring Lord. In both terms, God is portrayed as acting in judgment and righteousness with reference to the poor and meek.

There is no way to avoid seeing that this beautiful portion of scripture is imaging a rather drastic intention regarding God's view of things as they are and also as God intends they shall become.

God means for creation to extend into the future. It is to be a creation not only of things and objects, but also of values. This word points to a transformation of relationships and a transfer of power.

The words "and a little child shall lead them" is a modification of who shall be in charge. The social order is intended to reflect right-eousness and faithfulness. The exaggerated imagery of these verses makes the point vividly clear. We may cling to the present but God is announcing a new design for the future. The peace set forth is within an environment of changed relationships based on a new standard of values.

What more exciting news can there be at Christmastime for an unsettled world? The issue is whether Christmas will be an occasion to observe or, on the other hand, does Christmas describe an age that is coming? If it is to be the latter, we are invited to become Christmas people who embody the presence of God in Jesus Christ in our decisions for living.

Peace: God with Us

There are a couple of catchy insights in Luke 2 as the account of the birth of Jesus is told. One is that the shepherds were afraid of the spiritual presence around them when an angel of the Lord appeared.

The reason I am attracted to this feature of the story is that it is so much like all of us. We are in the fields, stores, shops, and offices doing our job. Probably we do not see ourselves as being anyone of importance. In fact, that may be a problem of ours.

Then one day we are aware of a spiritual dimension to life. It may be a fresh awareness that life is more than it appears to be. There is the reality of God. That can be frightening or it can be reassuring. It depends on our response.

Anyway, the shepherds went to Bethlehem as they were told to do. They saw Jesus. A new spirit came over them. They went back to their fields, "glorifying and praising God for all they had heard and seen."

I don't think life was ever the same again. They had experienced reformation and conversion. Life, they knew, has a divine dimension.

The shots are really not called by Caesar Augustus. They are ultimately called by God. Peace and confidence were gifts by Another.
They still are.

Peace is a word that is very much with us these days. For Christians this means that God is with us. That is the core, the heart, the
center of our search for Peace. Peace is here in Jesus Christ. To the
extent that we make Him visible in our relationships with one
another and in the family of nations, we are the people of God.

Blessed Christmas to you. Blessed Peace to you and to all people
of the earth.

Do We Miss the Message?

The sands of December are falling away and there is much to do
to prepare for Christmas. As usual at our house, gifts must still be
purchased. Cards are to be sent.

We concern ourselves with so many things which have so little
to do with the meaning of Christmas. The birth of Christ was harsh
but gentle; cruel but gracious; weak but bountiful with strength. If
we were to know what Christmas means we would spend more
time pondering these things and sharing our insights with one
another.

There were shepherds. They would be helpless at the mall. Joseph
and Mary were without even a modest motel. How could such a
meaningful event have occurred in a stable? Actually, the people
who were just people did the best they could and with their participation the great event was ushered in.

The culprit was Herod, who was the "guy in charge." His gov-
ernance, like much governmental administration today, was not for
the purpose of doing right for its own sake. It was to keep control.
How can one observe Christmas and stay in control as a person, as
a nation? Naturally, the answer is that you can't. Someone else has
come to be in control by making us free.

The shepherds came to worship. Herod connived. The wise men
brought gifts. Herod was determined to undo God. It was a test of
wills.

Which is the most real in the Christmas event, angels or Herod's power? Certainly the Herods are more real. But folks, if we believe in the Herods of the world more than we do in the angels, we are the losers because the angels win whether or not they are real.

Now there is something to think about. The weak are not supposed to be strong, but Christmas says they are. The ones without status have no standing, yet they have permanence in the Christmas hymns and traditions.

The losers who came to worship Jesus are the winners. The winners who stand with Herod are the losers. Truth alone is the gift. It is only Jesus who is real along with those who join His realness and become as human as He is. He was so blessedly human He was divine. Therein lies the gift for us, in us, that makes us sacred in our being human.

I've got to think about all this, but it makes our frantic efforts seem empty. We may make the deadline but miss the message.

Christmas Still Packs a Punch

Many of us can look wistfully on the way Christmas was in previous times. If such sentimental memories remain, these provide a gift that isn't all bad. In fact, good memories, though sentimental, can provide benchmarks of that which is worthwhile in Christmas. Most of the fond memories one would like to reclaim are filled with the simple things—love, family, special gatherings, smells, surprises.

The meaning of Christmas remains a substantial component in lives that recall or otherwise discover that life's essentials have to do with quality of relationships. It is also when we are aware of that, Christmas is as meaningful now as fifty years ago.

On the other hand, if Christmas is an institutionalized experience alone, whose emphasis impacts us from either commercial motivation to buy happiness, or to hawk the virtues of love and kindness through routine religious marketing routines, we still miss the mark.

Focus the camera of the soul on the lifestyle of Christ and you will see and celebrate what matters. It will be a radical change from the way we view one another usually. It focuses on love, the right to be an individual free of exploitation, and the notion that happiness is in the long run achieved by giving of oneself to another and understanding the other person's predicament.

Christmas hasn't lost its punch. It changes some people even for a while. Others retain the crust of Herod if not through Christmas, then when Christmas is over.

The fondest memories I have of Christmases past are those one doesn't put in a box or ring up on the cash register. If one has had the benefit of the gifts without price—love, family, smells, times when imagination won out over reality—these carry one through to a meaningful Christmas season.

Christmas has become too institutionalized by commerce and has been oversentimentalized by organized religion. Neither form in extreme is healthy.

The birth of Jesus was the beginning of one of the most radical lives ever to appear. When we treat one another as Jesus did, we know we have seen God. But that birth also tells us that such a life is costly and sometimes unpopular.

For those who catch the notion that Christmas means love is better than hate, giving better than receiving, and living together in peace is an imperative, Christmas has an ongoing life-ordering effect that time doesn't phase.

Jesus—The Prince of Peace

Jesus came into the world hunted and hated even as a baby. The marginal people (shepherds) were the first to hear the announcement of his birth. He was born in a stable where no one in a self-respecting family would be found. And yet, there were those who saw in Him the hope of their lives.

Immediately, the principalities and powers were after Him. Faithful parents nurtured and protected Him in infancy. Even the expectancy for what and who He might be threatened organized religion and organized government.

What He represented was a new order—a new approach to the

value of persons and to first loyalties. It was clear from the outset that, if it were believed He had been sent from God, the scale of priorities would be turned upside down.

Jesus never got out from under the threat that He posed to the world as it was. The danger followed Him from within His religion and from within the governmental values of the time.

His was a costly birth, a costly life, a costly death, and a redeeming resurrection. Thanks be to God for Christmas. Christ is still our hope.

At the heart of it not much has changed. Organized religion is still at odds with itself. The powers that shape society for all of us are unwilling to risk all the fulfillment of His peace.

Jesus came in peace. Jesus was the Prince of Peace. The proposition is still before us. What will we let Him do and be in the midst of our differences?

We have all been caught up in the meanness of "unpeace." Diabolic attitudes show up in church affairs as well as societal affairs. The birth of Jesus is still not accepted as practical in the so-called real world. Only those open to receiving and welcoming Him can make the needed difference.

Because of Jesus there is so much we can be and do; but first, He must be the Prince of Peace for each of us. When that is honestly faced, there is a merry Christmas awaiting us and the members of the global community.

Bishop Angelelli, in 1974 in Rome, on the occasion of the twenty-fifth anniversary of his priestly ordination, wrote the following:

> The mother country is bearing a child amid blood and pain . . .
> The evenings are shedding tears for that hope the child may be born without hatred and with love.
> My land is pregnant with life in this night of pain, as it waits for dawn to break and reveal a new person, Lord.

Elaine and I send our Christmas blessing for all our people. May the New Year see us drawing nearer to the joy of discovering a new person.

Christmas Gives Hope for a Happy New Year

Is there a time when Christmas is over? We may say that December 26 is that time. It may be when the presents have been opened. For ministers, we may breathe a sigh of relief when the candles are blown out and the lights are turned off after the Christmas Eve service. Then again, the pastor may feel that is when Christmas can really begin—when the sermons, the services of Advent and the Christmas programs, and Sunday School class parties are at an end. It is easy for such feelings and sighs of relief to overtake us.

However, there is a deeper sense in which Christmas is meant to be an experience that gives the New Year its meaning. In other words, Christmas is meant to be a full-time, year-round experience. Christ is born. He lives. The New Year is our opportunity to witness afresh to the living truth that God Almighty is real, present, powerful, loving, and responsible.

Should that be the case, and I believe it is, we are not alone. We can take chances in the New Year in faith. We can risk being witnesses to a life of Hope. We can be liberated to believe and strive for Peace as Peacemakers in the sense that Jesus taught and exemplified. We can be aggressive on behalf of Peace on earth and goodwill to all persons because the "I" that is each of us is attached to a "Thou" that is the glue holding life together.

The central mission of the church is to bring people into a saving relationship with Christ. All else follows. But something must "follow." We are called to live as the people of God, deciding, acting, and serving One whose world it is. We follow a Christ who from the day He was baby Jesus until He completed His earthly ministry was a refugee of sorts, a sojourner, who was never safe, secure, and out of harm's way. And yet, the world cannot transcend His style of peacemaking on the personal level or the global level. When we abandon that style we experience trouble and violence within and without.

The New Year offers a time of beginning again. We have reason to abandon old unfaith and take a fresh, vigorous hold on the future. Thus, there is every reason, especially for those who have an ongoing experience of Christmas, to say, "Happy New Year."

So, because Christ lives, "Happy New Year!" May the "I" that is each of us become the recipients of the "Thou" that is God. God is here. Division in the church and violence in the world can end. It must or else Herod will have caught Him.

CHAPTER
4

Bishop Business,
Part I

Holy Communion

Lord, in this Holy Communion celebration,
Let me be astounded by the reality of Christ.
In the broken bread, I see pierced hands.
In the poured out wine, I see life given for others—
      a body torn for others,
            blood poured out for others,
Is it my body that must be given?
Is it my blood that is called forth?
O Brother Christ, your claim and invitation
     is a call to live by dying,
        to keep by giving,
          to find by losing.
            KWH

Editor's note: The following two mentions are from an August
1976 edition of the *Arkansas Methodist* newspaper announcing the arrival of Bishop Hicks in his first assignment.

Official Welcome Planned for Arkansas's New Bishop

A Service of Acceptance for Bishop Kenneth W. Hicks, whose
assignment as resident bishop of the Arkansas Area of The United
Methodist Church became effective Sept. 1, has been scheduled for
early October. Details of the service are being planned by the Committees on the Episcopacy of the two Arkansas Area annual conferences. Bishop and Mrs. Hicks moved to Little Rock last Tuesday,
Aug. 24. They are making their home at the former Episcopal residence, 3909 South Lookout Street, which they are purchasing from
the area.

The Service of Acceptance, tentatively scheduled to be held at
First United Methodist Church in Little Rock within the first two
weeks of October, will be a worship service, ecumenical in nature,
with leaders of various denominations invited to participate.

To afford opportunity for United Methodists and friends
throughout the two Annual Conferences to become acquainted
with Bishop and Mrs. Hicks, a series of receptions will be scheduled
by the 13 districts of the conferences, following the initial Service
of Acceptance.

Bishop Hicks was one of four bishops elected at the South Central Jurisdictional Conference, held last July 13–15 at Lincoln, NE.
At the time of his election he was completing his third year as senior
pastor of Trinity United Methodist Church in Grand Island, NE.
He had previously served as superintendent of the Central District
of the Nebraska Conference, in addition to numerous pastoral
appointments in Nebraska and Colorado.

The Hicks have two children, Linda Diane, a speech pathologist
at West Nebraska General Hospital in Scottsbluff, NE, and Debra
Dawn, a senior at the University of Nebraska in Lincoln.

Bishop Hicks' offices are in the United Methodist Headquarters

Building, 715 Center Street, Little Rock, adjacent to First United Methodist Church. The headquarters building also houses offices of the Councils on Ministries of the two Annual Conferences, the Area Treasurer, the Little Rock District Superintendent and the *Arkansas Methodist.*

A Message from Bishop Hicks

To our new Friends in Arkansas:

We are about to begin a new journey together. As we have gathered the loose ends since July 15, the anticipated transition has been blessed with an outpouring of greetings and acts of graciousness beyond all deserving or expectation.

On his retirement from the Supreme Court, William O. Douglas wrote in a letter to his colleagues, "I am reminded of many canoe trips I have taken in my lifetime. Those who start down a water course may be strangers at the beginning but almost invariably are close friends at the end."

We will travel through rapids and carry loads around the falls, but surely God will place scenes of accomplishment, joy, and Christian fellowship along the way. Elaine and I have come to Arkansas eagerly. We felt right at home at the Arkansas breakfast at Jurisdictional Conference and knew then that this is where we belong. Pray for us. We will want you to be, not behind us, but beside us. Surely God has great days ahead for us all.

Kenneth W. Hicks

Christ's Covenant People

In a way, this will be my first General Conference. Oh yes, I've been to General Conference before, but never as a bishop. When you are a bishop, you go to General Conference automatically; but you don't vote because you can't. You won't speak in floor debate. You don't argue the merits or demerits of proposed legislation in a legislative committee—only delegates and occasional resource persons have that privilege.

So, I don't know just what bishops do at General Conference. There is some presiding, some devotional preaching, a communion service, and an Episcopal message from the Council of Bishops. I will give an address at the meeting of the United Methodist Rural Fellowship—but it is going to be different.

I have had several letters from people who feel that their bishop can influence some legislative decisions, but I'm afraid the opportunity is minimal.

Every petition, every letter goes before a legislative committee comprised of delegates chosen by the annual conference at the last session. Four ministers and four laypersons from each of our conferences will be in place when all of the voting takes place. They will be faithful representatives of Arkansas.

The issues will be many and, in many cases, thorny. Our church, by its nature, is varied and diverse. This will be reflected in the actions taken as approximately one thousand delegates, from all over the nation and the world, bring their convictions to the deciding process.

One thing stands out in my mind. The congregation of which we are members, whether in Arkansas or New York, is the place where we worship, marry, bury, baptize, and console. We are in covenant with that congregation and other congregations throughout the Church. We do not see eye to eye on all issues, but we are Christ's. The Church is His. We are His people. The members of the Church with whom we disagree are His people, too. The important thing is the COVENANT—that spiritual linkage we have in sharing the responsibility of being the Church. As Christ's followers, the spirit of Christ must be sought and lived out. The living of it will not be in the uniformity of our Christian expression, but in the covenant caring of and by the people who have Christ in common as Lord.

I believe we can offer our Church and the General Conference to God, and that God takes the risk with us as to the possibility of The United Methodist Church being a channel of His redemptive work. You and I can be as orthodox, as spiritual, and as evangelistic as we are led. We can be concerned about the well-being of the society around, if that is where we are led. The important thing is to remember that God in Christ has called us to be a congregation, a fellowship in covenant, that accepts and cares about that which unites; it cautions about that which divides and polarizes and is responsive to the aliveness of Christ still creating and making all things new.

Elaine and I will be in the Council of Bishops meeting from April 7 to April 13 in Nashville, Indiana. And then we are off to Indianapolis for the General Conference until April 25.

Pray for this conference. Pray for the delegates. Pray for The United Methodist Church. God is using our Church. He will continue to use it in exciting ways because it is His church and our opportunity to create with Him.

Unity in Christ, Not Uniformity

One major concern which has wrung out a great deal of anxiety and soul-searching on my past has been that of spiritual elitism. It is reflected not only in the Church, but in issues of society as well. It has to do with that condition in which one's religious views become characterized by sharp edges to our Christian expression, rather than round edges. Edges which cut, polarize, separate, and take on forms of exclusiveness leave me cold somehow, and even grief stricken, as one views in contrast the warmth and accepting nature of Christ.

I cannot quarrel with those who wish to be a congregation of people who think and believe alike, and who insist on conformity by those who enter the fellowship so that uniformity prevails. There are groups like that. Such position is their decision and their conviction. It does not happen to be The United Methodist positon.

Covenant is a great term which permeates the Bible from beginning to end. It began as God entered into covenant relationship with Israel to enable them to become a new people. The covenant was effective between God and the community or nation, not just God and individuals. As members of the covenant relationship they were expected to be responsible as a body and for the body. They were not to forsake each other. They were to care for each other. Each one "doing his own thing" was not God's way. They were to bear each other's burdens, share the suffering and the victories.

As *The Interpreter's Dictionary of the Bible* states, "The first-century Christian community was thus profoundly moved by the conviction that God has acted in a new way through Jesus Christ, a way which left them so completely in God's debt (Romans 8:12; I Corinthians 7:23) that their love for each other, for God, and for the world results from God's love for the world (I John 4:19). In this understanding, doing God's will flows out of God's loving relationship with mankind (Romans 14; I Corinthians 8), a relationship signaled and sealed by the Cross (Hebrews 4–10)."

Surely a part of being the church is the struggle and the adventure in the congregation of discovering the meaning of that covenant relationship in ways that are supportive, accepting, forgiving, and reconciling.

When the process of that journey reaches points at which polarization and divisiveness threaten the unity of the congregation, prayerful interchange and discussion must be considered holy agenda because unity with Christ is at stake. But if unity with Christ is uppermost, we do not have to be in uniformity with each other.

Ordinarily in biblical and church history, this tension as to what it means to be "the people of God" can be resolved. However, when polarization and division become the norm and the well-being of the congregation is threatened; when a state of division threatens to take permanent shape; when these matters are not resolved by the congregation itself, then, in our Church, it becomes the duty of the bishop, with the help of the district superintendents, to intervene so as to endeavor to bring wholeness once again to the covenant group.

Thus, the issue out front for the bishop is not basically theological (though differences in theology may have produced the situation). The issue is that of salvaging the covenant body so that the congregation can pursue its covenant journey of being in caring relationship with Christ and each other. The intention of "pluralism" in The United Methodist Church is not uniformity, but unity with Christ through diverse stances that are shared, respected, and translated into the call to join Christ in redeeming the world in which He resides.

Suggestions for the Future

The drought and heat of the summer will not soon be forgotten; in fact, it will be in our minds for some time to come. Because that is the case, we should face the future with hope and renewed faithfulness.

Congregations are beginning to plan for the year ahead. Each congregation should be asking, "What is God calling us to do?" The answer to that question, if it is specific enough, will constitute a major goal for the congregation to achieve in the months ahead.

Let me offer a few suggestions:

1. Look to the spiritual condition of our people—beginning with oneself. Is our faith a vibrant faith, or is it rather routine and colorless? This personal introspection is very important; because what we are in terms of the quality and vitality of our faith will be translated into the kind of congregation we have in our church.

2. Pray for your church locally and for The United Methodist Church around the world.

3. Emphasize the good things about our church. We are not positive enough. Too much attention is given to our weaknesses and to our faults as we see them in ourselves and each

other. It might not be a bad idea for each Administrative Board and Council on Ministries meeting to begin with a look at the good things that are taking place in our church.

4. Look for ways and occasions to reinforce and encourage your pastor. Many times the very busyness of the community causes the pastor to feel that the church has a secondary place. When this occurs, it is difficult for a pastor's morale to remain high. Tell him or her that they are doing well and that you are interested in your pastor's well-being.

5. Look for the good things our denomination is doing, as well as our annual conferences.

6. Be a participant and not just a critic that takes pot shots at the church from the outside. The place to change the church for the better is on the inside.

7. Pastors, be a teaching minister. Inform your people theologically. Do what you do with enthusiasm. Our people want help in understanding the great beliefs. Lead them in planning intentionally. Be specific in planning courses of actions. By such intentional effort, the congregation can be enabled to observe and evaluate achievements that have been taking place.

8. Let us win people to Christ and His church. If the church is exciting, the people will respond. Let our evangelism be directed toward the inactive, as well as the non-members. It is time we show increased membership. Revival needs to take place in our own concern about the relationship of people to Christ, and what they are, or are not, receiving in that relationship.

9. Show joy! Emphasize the positive. Let us all assume responsibility for the fellowship of Christ's body. Let there be evidence that Christ lives. May worship be celebration. Let us face the reality of sin in ourselves and the world and "give them Christ."

Laity Want to "Buy In"

Sitting in the pews of churches are believing laity whose theology is shaped by faith and life experiences that provide a unique message. The church needs to hear that witness. I am of the conviction that it should be done authentically by the lay speaker without the hang-ups of making it sound like a professional preacher; that the service of worship should not be conducted by laity as if they are playing preacher. It should be done with a heartfelt expression of those who have this rare privilege of leading fellow worshippers in a service of divine worship. It should be done without regard or fear that it will not be done as well as the pastor might do it.

Laity have something to say about God, and they have convictions about the meaning of faith in life that are unique to their setting. We all need that witness.

Now, let me go further and propose that in Arkansas United Methodism the laity do not have enough input into the factors that shape the local church and the Annual Conference.

We clergy tend to overwhelm by our professionalism, rather than enable the laity to see the church as an expression of faith in life. As I write this on the afternoon of Reformation Sunday, I am reminded that Protestantism believes in the priesthood of all believers. One of the top agenda items of the ordained clergy, and of the church generally, should be that of building quality into the ministry of all persons and of enabling laity to provide ministry also in the community—locally and in the world.

I have a distinct impression that laity want to learn the message of the scripture and want to have insight into what this means as to their life and society in general. Laity want the church to be effective. They have some positive ideas about this, if they can have a chance to buy into the enterprise. "Buying into the enterprise" means more than paying apportionments and salaries. It has to do with helping establish the priorities, the programs, and the overall mission with which we are charged as Christians.

The task we face is diminished when we do not communicate

meanings and intentions. The meaning and intention of the apportionments are as essential as the payment of the apportionments.
The meaning and intention of the programs of the church are as
essential as voting them into being. If these meanings and intentions
are not shared, then we have not communicated well. Part of the
reason for this lack of understanding is that we are content to be
vague, yes, and even content to sound spiritual.

I hear our laity asking that we be specific in what we do. They
want to know why an enterprise is worth the price tag that is on
it. We are all ministers, laity included. If we clergy do not appreciate
this, we need to look at our heritage again.

Do we dare risk being positive about this?

If we know our Christ, we can afford to be positive, for there is
a church to create and a world to win.

We who work in the matters of the church from day to day don't
realize how much we need to involve and inform the laity. I have
said before that I believe our laity want to see the church move with
vitality toward being the people of God.

The church will be healthy to the extent that the laity share the
plans, provide input in the intentions, and participate in the action
as co-owners of what is done.

The term *lay member* of the Annual Conference is an important
one. In reality these persons are not delegates representing a local
church, but members of the conference. They come, not obligated
to vote according to the mandate of the congregation, but to vote
their conscience in keeping with what they believe to be the good
of the conference.

Thanks for Local Pastors

A special word of appreciation needs to be said of our Local Pastors. Over one hundred of these dedicated persons serve churches
in Arkansas Conferences. By definition a Local Pastor is a layperson
approved by the ministerial members in full connection in an
Annual Conference who is authorized to perform all the duties of
a pastor, including the Sacraments, while assigned to a particular

charge under the specific supervision of a counseling elder, subject to annual renewal.

An important feature for all of us to realize is the preparation that is necessary to be a Local Pastor. A five-year course of study is required under the Division of Ordained Ministry of our denomination. Except for unusual circumstances, the normal expectation is that this course will be completed within eight years if they are full-time pastors. This means that these persons go to a seminary each summer, where the course is offered, to spend a month in study in order to remain qualified.

Regarding this, a word to churches is appropriate. This is required preparation for the pastor. It is not vacation time. The expense for a supply to care for the pulpit while the pastor is away is not the pastor's responsibility.

We do not have enough fully trained pastors who have gone the full college and seminary route. Even if we did, there are many churches who would not have pastoral leadership available were it not for the Local Pastors. Most of them serve at least two, and often more, small membership churches.

We must continue to provide support structures such as skill and morale building events and cooperative ministries relationships to enhance and maximize the effectiveness of these servants and their congregations.

A Cooperative Venture to Celebrate the Spirit

Holly Grove is a small town in Monroe County that's not just another small town; at least, it wasn't on a Sunday evening in late June. There is a unique air to it even as you drive into town. Maybe the word is "pride." We drove down the main drag to the "Bent Rail," the name of the restaurant that is housed in the attractive old depot. The place where the railroad used to be gives the street a spaciousness, partly because the space is intentionally cared for. As we winged off in either direction for a few blocks, one couldn't help but to be impressed by the homes both old and new. The old ones catch your eye because so many of them are kept in mint condition. You can imagine yourself in an Arkansas version of Williamsburg.

Representatives from twelve United Methodist congregations met at the church for a 5:30 light supper in the churchyard. The churches represented were Taylor's Chapel, Wesley Chapel, Cotton Plant, Hunter, Holly Grove, Shiloh Shrine, Brinkley, Brasfield, Clarendon, Cornerstone, Wheatley, and Salem. It seemed like the whole town had been mowed for our coming, but I suspect each weekend finds the town a new haircut.

A cluster of twelve churches are in an unwritten covenant relationship finding ways of cooperating with one another to achieve a new experience in being the church. After supper we had worship with participation from all the pastors, along with a bell choir, and choirs and musicians from the participating churches. The church was full, the singing was fervent and, helped by the visit and supper on the grounds preceding the service, a community was evident that is not geographical but one of the spirit.

I had the feeling that each of those churches felt strong rather than weak, hopeful rather than discouraged, and that therein lies part of the answer to the future of small membership churches—and larger ones, too. As congregations and pastors worship and serve together cooperatively, a new creation is formed by the way of what the church is about, and a new experience of ministry is realized that maximizes the strengths of each person and each unit.

It wouldn't be a bad model for the world; but then, the Gospel has been saying that all along.

Beliefs/Relationships: Experiencing the Christ

My relationship with Christ has been an encounter, not once, but many times. I could recount many times when I have been moved to tears of awareness of His presence; sometimes alone, at other times with others. My experience with Christ has, thankfully, contained more content of experience than belief. It has manifested itself often—sometimes too often—as a call to respond.

God's pure goodness came in Jesus. When God is given birth,

whether in church or in other venues, He is always pure goodness. I have been most vividly blessed by His visitation in relationships. If the will to believe blends with a knowledge of His being in relationships, it is good. If the blend does not occur, if belief does not change relationships or vice versa, it seems to me that Christ is somehow omitted.

I never cease to be amazed at the intensity with which some people form beliefs about Christ that leave relationships untouched, maybe even cruelly isolated as a result of judgmental legalistic beliefs.

Scripture has the ability to point the way to places and situations where Christ is likely to be found. Sometimes I miss seeing Him. Sometimes I look in the wrong places, the wrong issues. So does my church.

I can't get very excited about proving that I have Him, or He has me. I make no claim that my faith is more authentic than the faith of another. There have been numberless times when I have known glimpses of the full-grown Master as Lord and as Friend.

His pedigree will not save me, but His nature and His unique expression of living as a human aware of God does. He points me in a direction with His style and manner of life.

Sometimes I wish He would let me just be a believing Christian. Instead, His way of being a person and His way of showing responsibility to His Father points to injustice, hunger, unemployment, and the threat of war so dramatically that I know my faith would be sterile were I to withhold taking a position at times. The fact that self-satisfied advocates occasionally seek to impose a narrow legalism upon others was not unknown to Jesus; it can't be to the others of us who take His resurrection seriously.

I believe that creation continues. God is a God of history. I believe the history we are making holds Him who judges, loves, redeems, and invites.

Can't we let it go at that and learn to love Him by loving His creation and His creatures, and by caring for them in a world that still is on its way toward His intention?

When God confronted Cain following the killing of his brother, God asked Cain two questions, "Where is your brother?" and "What have you done?" Is He still asking us those questions regarding our world today? A willingness to deal with these two questions would identify us as an enlightened people far more that some of our religious pursuits.

Religious people tend to spend too much time answering questions God hasn't asked! Maybe that's why our witness doesn't ring true.

The Appointment-Making Process

Probably the most exhausting and sometimes excruciating work that is done by the bishop and district superintendents is that of appointment making. By description in *The Discipline* and by tradition in our church it is the uppermost responsibility of the bishop to fix the appointments of our ministers. There is nothing in the job description of the episcopacy that is so singularly set forth and descriptive of the role of the bishop.

Given that fact, the process becomes a priority responsibility. The making of appointments is viewed with seriousness by all bishops, but is appreciated in varied ways, depending in part on the nature of the bishop. For most of us it is not a fun time. When it is over and the appointments are ready for announcement, there may be relief and more especially a sense of satisfaction that the assignments have been given the best attention and judgment they could receive.

At this time of year our cabinets usually meet for at least two days or more at a time. We begin by having each district superintendent appraise the entire cabinet of the status of each appointment as it now stands. Indicated on our worksheets which we all have is various information as to the number of years the pastor has been at the present charge, the classification or relationship the pastor has with the conference, abbreviations indicating the level of importance as to whether the pastor stays or moves, and the salary the charge is now paying.

This process takes hours, sometimes days. The known input from churches and pastors is shared. Then we begin the process of matching profiles of pastors and churches.

There are many occasions when the ideal pastor is noted for a given situation. But there may be reasons why such a matching cannot take place at this time. A pastor may be in the midst of a critical phase of the life of the church where he or she now is. There are family considerations to take into account. In nearly all cases, to make an appointment means that another pastor must move over. The exceptions are those situations marked as "open," meaning the pastor is retiring, ministry has been terminated, or a death has occurred. Otherwise, it comes down to the reality that every appointment, every change, has the potential of affecting every pastor and every church in the conference.

"Consultation" is a word that has come into the vocabulary of appointment making by the law of the church and by common sense. In a connectional church, which is ours, consultation means in a practical sense that we discuss with Pastor Parish Relations Committees the needs of the local church or churches in the charge. It is important that we have as clear an understanding of those as possible. We talk with pastors about their situation and what we propose. Consultation does not mean that pastors are chosen or appointments are made on the basis of whether or not a majority consent is present in the church regarding a particular pastor. Nor does it mean that the pastor has the last word in whether or not an assignment is made. Churches "receive" a pastor that has been "sent." This is an important concept!

The time comes in the process when the cabinet agrees, on the basis of the consultations, that an assignment is to be made. A selection is agreed upon and this becomes the appointment.

It should be obvious that the process results in the best that can be arranged. It is not always the ideal. We have few ideal pastors and few ideal churches. The pastor ultimately appointed is a human being assigned to a church or churches that are composed of human beings. But every pastor must be appointed somewhere, and every church must finally have someone who is the pastor or at least responsible for pastoral functions. The latter minimal description applies to those situations where a temporary arrangement is made while a permanent arrangement is pending.

In cabinet meetings we can usually stay with this process of consideration for no more than about two hours, then a break is taken for a little breather. Phone calls are made in many of those breaks and meetings are arranged with Pastor Parish Relations Committees or with pastors.

We usually begin at 9 A.M. unless it is the first day of our meeting. Ordinarily, by 6 P.M. we know we have had a day of it.

We begin our sessions with devotions. We quarrel, we argue, we consult. Eventually, we decide. That decision is shared with the parties involved. By the middle of May we look forward to having our work ready for conference. In each situation, the bishop has the responsibility to say, in effect, "on the basis of what we know and what we have, this will be the appointment."

Sometimes we hit a snag and have to start over. The resulting process, though, means that we work through Pastor Parish Relations Committees. It is crucial that these committees are representative of the congregations. The result is leadership—pastoral leadership. The process must be about the hardest work there is because it is both human and divine. I just thought you might want to know that this is what we are doing as conscientiously as we can these days. Somehow, with cooperation of people and the blessing of God, it works. But, just the same, pray for us.

Annual Conference: Always Another Chance

Annual Conference is one of the experiences of human existence that defies total explanation. In fact, to an outsider I suppose it might make no sense at all. But we keep doing it—having Annual Conference that is. And wonder of wonders, some things get done. A few issues become resolved, assignment of pastors is made, some programs of ministry are adopted along with budgets. It is amazing what tenaciousness United Methodists have as they endure this ponderous, yet participatory way of getting things done. There is enough machinery, momentum, and organizational structure in place to (as Dr. Francis Christie says) assure that The United Methodist Church will go on long after Christianity has disappeared from the face of the earth.

I suppose that humorous remark takes into account the thought that it might take two hundred years just to dismantle the church and to stop the mail from coming. On the other hand, sometimes it seems that United Methodism must be plugged into the computer system that runs Little Rock's traffic light system. Still the traffic moves, and so do we.

An Annual Conference is always determining its identity. This is done in part by the nature and quality of its decisions. Annual Conference always gives us another chance to do better.

A Favorite of Mine: "'Twas the Night After . . ."

'Twas the night after Conference, and all over the state
There arose a great clamor for boxes and crates;
The Lord had called, the Bishop behooved;
So Methodist preachers were again on the move.
Ma and Pa quite happy, the children so gay—
Had all settled down for an indefinite stay.
When in the church board there arose such a clatter
The D.S. had to come to see what was the matter.
Away to the meetin' house he flew like a flash
To hear all the "pros" and "cons" rehashed.
The "pros" wore smiles, their praises were loud;
The "agins" had faces like great thunderclouds.
There was old money-bags so lively and quick,
I knew in a moment he had raised the "old nick."
The D.S. acted with ease and dispatch;
So what happened? They moved, natch!
The children were summoned from school and their games;
Pa whistled and shouted and called them by name:
"Come Johnnie, come Mary, come Martha and Dan—
Come Susan, come Esther, come Wesley and Ann—
Pack up your possessions, from attic to hall,
Now dash away, dash away, dash away all."
To all parts of the house they ascended like rockets,
And I watched them as they unscrewed lightbulbs from their
sockets.
With fiendish delight they corralled pet and toys,
And established a record for long-sustained noise!
Their eyes, how they glistened! Their dimples, how merry!
"Isn't it fun to move, Mummy?"
"Oh yes, it is, very!"
The dishes were wrapped, the books placed in neat rows,
(They had been that way for weeks, I suppose.)

There were pictures and mirrors, pots and pans;
Those movers would have to work like Trojans.
After quite some delay I heard on the drive
A sound that told me the van had arrived.
There was a driver, and helpers so slow
I was sure they would never get ready to go.
A bundle of burlap he had slung over his back,
And by this sign indicated he was ready to pack.
They poke things into the cavernous depth
Until the house looked quite bereft.
At long last they finished and slammed shut the door—
But wait a minute—there are a few things more.
No room inside, so tied to the tail
Were bed springs, ladders, and an old garbage pail.
Then off went the van with chattels and goods,
The children's bicycle tied to the hood.
Pa spoke not a word, but went straight to work,
Put the family in the car, then turned with a jerk,
And looking once more at the church he must leave
Raised his hand in salute—he would not grieve.
He jumped in the car, turned on the ignition,
And away they all flew to their newly found mission.
But I heard him exclaim ere they drove out of sight,
"This time I hope God and the Bishop are right!"
                    Author unknown

The Standard Is Excellence at Our Children's Home!

Editor's note: When the bishop wrote this, a bill was in process before the Arkansas Legislature, which would exempt certain child-care facilities from state review. This was part of his response.

With regard to child care and the church, it seems to me that we should strive toward the highest of standards, particularly at the point of those disciplines and policies that treat the behavioral dimensions of a child's personality. The church should set the standard.

There are some expressions of caring for children that are clearly not acceptable and not in the interests of the dignity of the child emotionally or physically. There is a responsibility on the part of society to see that the best interests of children who do not have personal families or homes are carried out.

I speak only of the United Methodist agencies when I say that I believe the church should lead the way in quality care of human life of whatever age. Children should be cared for by the best standards we can afford, and by those standards which are in keeping with an understanding that children are persons who have too few advocates. The church performs a service in its institutions of human care, but should not conduct that care in a manner which seeks exemption from public scrutiny and from generally accepted guidelines.

I am happy that our United Methodist Children's Home has sought not only compliance with state regulations, but also accreditation by nationally recognized bodies. Our child-care centers located in church facilities are endeavoring to apply recognized standards for such enterprise, not to comply, but to be responsible. I'm glad.

To All Who Work for the Church: "Your Labor Is Not in Vain"

I want to take off my hat to the many people who are helping the church to work and have meaning at all levels, including the local congregation. It happens because people committed to Christ really care. There are obstacles. There is tension. Financial resources are modest. I have observed what groups of committed Christians can provide in ideas, service, designs for action, and verbal Christian witness.

Yes, we are engaged as Christians in creation. Whoever you are, wherever you are as you read this, know that your efforts are not in vain. We meet God in the arenas of human experience and proclaim Him and endeavor to make Him evident. That is tiring and hard work most of the time, but it is part of our proclamation in word and deed.

Thank you, whoever you are, for sharing the pain and struggle in giving birth to Christlikeness. Yours is a joy of depth and substance.

Editor's note: In August of 1984 after having served eight years in the episcopacy for the two United Methodist Conferences of the Arkansas Area, Bishop Kenneth Hicks was appointed to serve in the episcopacy for the state of Kansas. The following is his final column in the Arkansas United Methodist newspaper in his role of the bishop of Arkansas.

Shalom!

This is the last piece I will write for this spot as your bishop. It is the toughest to compose. What parting thoughts should be shared? How does one say "thank you" adequately for an eight-year spiritual pilgrimage with the wonderful people of Arkansas?

We can never be the same, nor would we want to be the same. The eight years have been too experience-filled, too person-filled, too intimately shared through thick and thin. The result has been an evolvement into a spiritual entity shaped by opportunities, problems, encounters, dreams, failures, and successes offered by so many with whom we have walked together. Of course then, one does not have that blending of intense living without being different as we approach the point of departure. We carry with us so much of what and who you have been to us.

At the reception at Hendrix on July 28, our hearts were so overcome with the gracious outpouring and the so very generous gift. It was not a gift deserved but a grace given and received. We have received from you, our friends, so much more than we have given during our time together.

You received us when we had no Episcopal experience. You gave Elaine and me a chance. It was given as a trust. We have done what we could to honor that trust. I can truly say, "My people made me a bishop." Thank you for generous and patient hearts. Thank you for the gracious farewell gift. Elaine went to the bank on Monday after the reception on Saturday and paid off a second mortgage—an improvement loan we took out a few years ago on our home.

As we come down to the last days, we realize how many there are with whom we would like to share a personal word. I guess such unfinished relationships are like a compass that never reveals the end of the trip, but only the direction that is without end.

As many of you know, my faith is of the sort that believes Christ is present in the world. Therefore, spiritual decisions are always made in the context of the human predicament. That's why I have never been able to separate religion from the social setting. Instead of the church withdrawing from the so-called secular scene, I think the church should be more evident in that arena than it is insofar as its impact is concerned.

What a politician believes politically is fraught with his or her religious values; thus that politician's vote is a faith or value statement most of the time and requires the church's notice. I do not know whether obedience to Christ will result in a large or smaller membership. I only know that God intends us to be faithful in proclamation and witness. What the result will be numerically is hard to forecast. Evangelism without social conscience is maintenance. Evangelism with social conscience is transforming. In my heart I hold that ultimately the latter, in the long haul, will result in strength and growth.

A word about your new Episcopal family. Bishop and Mrs. Richard Wilke (Dick and Julia) are warm and able persons. They will bring a fresh perspective to Arkansas. Grant them the support and love you have given us and their leadership will bear fruit. Bishop Wilke brings a wealth of experience out of a distinguished ministry. When he asks your counsel, tell him how it is, not what you think he wants to hear. He is eager and creative. You will find in these fine people vision and dedication.

In the meantime, Elaine and I will carry blessed memories and continuing relationships to the broad blue skies of Kansas. Kansas is a strong United Methodist state. Its membership and geography represent larger responsibility. Thus we desire your prayers as we anticipate with excitement our assignment there.

We look forward to seeing your faces again. Our address will be: 6841 S.W. Dunstan Court, Topeka, Kansas 66610. "What would life be without packing boxes?" We hope to know soon.

SHALOM!

I Believe . . .

I believe that Jesus wanted to tap the achievable
    in every situation and every person.
There was something in Jesus that was above the political,
    the expedient, the sure thing.
He was always proposing the unusual,
    touching that which had always been untouched.
He wanted to help people reach higher
    than they had ever reached.
He first chose twelve, then seventy were chosen.
Now He stretches across time and touches us to try the untried,
    To achieve the unachievable.
The issue comes down to whether or not
    we will cooperate with Him;
        Or compete with each other.
I wonder which He wants us to do in our churches,
    in our ministries.
        Or do I already know?
        KWH

CHAPTER 5

Prayer, Hope, and Healing

Remember to Pray

I have heard it said, "when all else fails, remember to pray." I would like to suggest a more aggressive route. When you have prayed first, success or failure takes on a different significance. Often times, both success and failure require strength. Both are part of life. Both are in the experience of total living.

We used to hear of people who had a prayer list to which they referred each day. Such a practice is still relevant and still effective. Much of the unsettledness in today's living is due to the lack of a strong center. Sometimes we call the building of that center "spiritual formation." There are many important things, even crucial ones, as well as personal predicaments with which we can deal more adequately when they have been dealt with prayerfully.

Compose a prayer for yourself to use daily for one week. Maybe next week you will need to write another. Perhaps one week it will be a rather private personal prayer. Next week it may include the world.

This week, the following has been my prayer. It's not as good as your own, and next week I will try to do another one. I know I will want it to be more inclusive. But for now, here goes . . .

Through ten thousand prayers
    I have waded the infested waters of doubt.
The waves of overwhelming unknowing
    have diluted my certain faith until I say,
"O God, who ought to be, I press on—a foot slogger Christian."
    I have no other direction.
No other markings exist to make the journey
    than those blazed by a zealous, selfless Christ.
As He goes before me, an unseen but present Brother and Friend,
    I somehow know I am not alone.

So, Lord, when the way is unclear,
    when fog comes in over the meadows

of comfortable certainty, and I must pass through,
Reinforce my stride so that my faltering will not lead
    to surrender the darkness.

In the silence, when my unknowing needs to know,
    I wait for God.
My one certain resource, Hope, is my one true possession.
    That becomes a rock, a fortress.
When I cannot go forward,
    at least I have a place to stand.
Though fearful, my faith is unshaken.

Whether I am delivered, honored, or defeated,
    that reality rests on Him;
For God is my rock, my refuge, and my guide.
                    KWH

Public Prayer

I believe in prayer. Probably most of those who read this believe
in prayer. When our daughters were younger and were facing a test
at school, Elaine or I would quite often suggest that if they were
tense just before the exam, they could ask God to grant them peace
of mind and the gift to use the maximum knowledge they had in
their minds. Sometimes we would suggest that they utter a word of
thanks to God for that Presence and Love that surround us.

We tried to teach them that prayer is not necessarily a verbal exercise one must do aloud. One can think prayers and communicate in
silent verbiage as one carries out the responsibilities of the day.

My point is that the act of praying does not require an Act of
Congress. One does not have to have a legislative approval to pray.
Congress does not make prayer possible or real (unless by the stan-
dards of that body it has to be certain that prayer is done "right").

For civil authority to sanction prayer imposes on prayer itself a
philosophy or thought system which seems to say that prayer is not

a prayer unless a legal time is available, and that prayer is predetermined by characteristics preformed by a mandated authority. The assumption implied is that civil legislative groups know the appropriate ways of expressing one's prayer style.

The Supreme Court allows one to pray. And even if it didn't, how does the Supreme Court or the United States Congress know whether or not one is praying? Have you ever prayed while looking into someone's face? You might try it. It can even affect relationships.

For our political leaders to assume that there is no praying possible as things now stand, and to propose to correct that by governmental definitions has to be viewed as an imposition of civil religion, or a shortsighted understanding of the nature of prayer or both.

Prayer that has to be seen, heard, legalized, or prescribed is an unpleasant reminder of the model of the Pharisees, one rejected by Jesus. It assumed that prayer has to be, at least, visible to be real.

I am bothered by this fostering of a theology of prayer that is limited in nature, at best, and grandstanding to public appeal, at worst. It might be comforting and helpful to a teacher to suggest to a class that there might be value amidst the din of the classroom exchange to have an occasion when the class might bask in a few moments of treasured silence. I wouldn't object to this, but I view this as classroom technique. For Congress, however, to formalize this moment into sanctioned prayer time is something else. What is the intended purpose? Someone wants to do something to somebody, if not in current legislation, then in legislation to come. I don't like the overtones or the undertones of it. There is more to come if such laws are passed.

If a child has been taught to pray, he or she can pray now. Congressional action doesn't make it so. The nature of prayer makes it so.

Proposed public prayer may be good politics, but it's faulty religion. Our people should know there is a difference.

"Strengthening the Soul" Is Basic to All Else

A recent scripture selection in the Lectionary was from Psalm 138. Verse 3 says, "On the day I called, thou didst answer me, my strength of soul thou didst increase." That verse hit me where I live for two reasons. One is that a disproportionate part of my praying is probably related to things, conditions, and personal problems. The second is that the greatest deficiency I see in myself is "strength of soul."

But I see myself in a lot of company. The thought surfaces that this is at the core of much of the instability in family life, international relations, crime and how to deal with it, and even our economy.

It is a question of identity. The fiber of being human and surviving it, dealing with a future that isn't what it used to be, the inner health that causes people to be survivors in the face of great odds; all of these longings were gathered by the writer of Psalm 138 and focused, not on the uncertainty, but on the reality of God. "Though I walk in the midst of trouble, thou dost preserve my life ..."

I get the feeling that by the time David wrote this he was a mature believer who knew that come what may, "thy steadfast love, O Lord, endures forever." His closing supplication is that God not forsake what he has begun.

Tucked away in the spirit as well as the words of this Psalm is the agenda for the local church. "Strengthening the soul" is basic to all else. Until that has been experienced, our budgets, goals, Sunday School classes, and sermons will have a hollow ring to them.

The Psalmist faces reality, sure enough. He talks of the lowly, the haughty, and even the wrath of his enemies. No simple Gospel for him. He even believes there is a purpose which the Lord has for him.

I don't know if the Lord has a future for The United Methodist Church as he wants it to become. That may be with more members or less; with a social concern as it is or with drastic alterations. But there is an intention for our church, for you, for me.

A major focus of attention must first be on "the strength of soul thou didst increase." Given that, we cannot lose and we cannot be defeated, and we can be faithful. Paul said it another way. "Faith, Hope, and Love, these abide."

Whoops! There's that challenge to face the reality of change again. I wonder, if I have strength of soul, what differences in priorities must occur?

Thought and Prayer Urged

The issue of abortion has been opened for discussion and decision by action of the Supreme Court. This matter deserves prayerful and considered thinking by all Christians as well as by the populace as a whole. Deep and sincere convictions run through this stream of human experience that contain opposite views. To the extent that is possible, emotions need to give way to responsible reflection in the context of life's sacredness.

Following is the position of our United Methodist Church as approved by the last (2008) General Conference. It is to be found in *The Book of Discipline*, Paragraph 161(J):

> *Abortion*—The beginning of life and the ending of life are the God-given boundaries of human existence. While individuals have always had some degree of control over when they would die, they now have the awesome power to determine when and even whether new individuals will be born. Our belief in the sanctity of unborn human life makes us reluctant to approve abortion.
>
> But we are equally bound to respect the sacredness of the life and well-being of the mother and the unborn child.
>
> We recognize tragic conflicts of life with life that may justify abortion, and in such cases we support the legal option of abortion under proper medical procedures. We support parental, guardian, or other responsible adult notification and consent before abortions can be performed on girls who have not yet reached the age of legal adulthood. We cannot affirm abortion as an acceptable means of birth control, and we unconditionally reject it as a means of gender selection.

We oppose the use of late-term abortion known as dilation and extraction (partial-birth abortion) and call for the end of this practice except when the physical life of the mother is in danger and no other medical procedure is available, or in the case of severe fetal anomalies incompatible with life. Before providing their services, abortion providers should be required to offer women the option of anesthesia.

We call all Christians to a searching and prayerful inquiry into the sorts of conditions that may cause them to consider abortion.

The Church shall offer ministries to reduce unintended pregnancies. We commit our Church to continue to provide nurturing ministries to those who terminate a pregnancy, to those in the midst of a crisis pregnancy, and to those who give birth.

We particularly encourage the Church, the government, and social service agencies to support and facilitate the option of adoption. (See ¶ 161.L.) We affirm and encourage the Church to assist the ministry of crisis pregnancy centers and pregnancy resource centers that compassionately help women find feasible alternatives to abortion.

Governmental laws and regulations do not provide all the guidance required by the informed Christian conscience. Therefore, a decision concerning abortion should be made only after thoughtful and prayerful consideration by the parties involved, with medical, family, pastoral, and other appropriate counsel.

Many of our people are asking what the position of our church is. This is the only official position we have as a denomination. It is not drawn in great detail. It simply states that we believe there are circumstances in which abortion is appropriate. It should be noted that implied is the reality that under some conditions an abortion should be considered but never casually, always seriously in view of the sacredness of life, as it pertains to both the baby and the mother. This position does not state that abortion is never justified. It does state that thoughtful and prayerful consideration by the parties involved, with appropriate counsel being part of the decision, is to be expected.

As with many other issues, our salvation requires the deepest inquiry in forming our opinions. We must not approach this matter with rancor toward others or with disregard to the mother. The boundaries of human existence are God-given, but as with most things God gives, we have a duty to use God-given minds in order to embrace each circumstance in which life finds itself in a responsible Christian way. We also believe in the freedom to develop our convictions as we believe God's expectation intends with compassion and love.

The Power of Hope

Lately, I have been reading about hope. I have found considerable help in a book by Walter Brueggemann entitled *Hope within History*. One notices that on numerous occasions, biblical characters seeking signs of hope within themselves were at times in the position of being rather isolated in their predicament because they were alone by being the only one of whatever they were. Sometimes it was a prophet, sometimes a king. There usually aren't many of that kind in one place, but I suppose even God would like to talk some things over with someone at times, because God is one of a kind.

If one will let the Bible help, and the Holy Spirit as well, there can be some new experiences of hope realized. It may take some looking, some praying and reflection. I know that.

Also, one has to look beyond institutionalized religion to find hope in history. Sometimes one will find it in the institutionalized church. It is intended by God to be there, but the Creator, being the risking one that God is, chose to place the organized church in human hands—even the proclamation of the Gospel story. Sometimes I think that God finds hope in the interchange with us human types who question, doubt, and respond in supplication.

The Psalm writer in the tenth Psalm rips into God with all eight cylinders and verbalizes his despair with fellow human beings with even cruel thoughts to the extent of proposing the breaking the arms of the evildoer. Naughty Psalmist!

But take note! The hopelessness of the writer was addressed to the reality of God and to the imperfect reality which was perceived by the believer. He believed God was foot-dragging and stonewalling, but God was still God.

Glory to all that's holy, a soul-saving therapy was encountered to the extent that the bitterness dissolved into an affirmation of faith:

O Lord, you will hear the desire of the meek;
you will strengthen their heart, you will incline your ear
to do justice for the orphan and the oppressed,
so that those from earth may strike terror no more.
    Psalm 10:17–18

Hope was restored in the midst of despair.

Brueggemann suggests that "hope reminds us not to absolutize the present, not to take it too seriously, not to treat it too honorably, because it will not last." He also reminds us that the function of hope is to "provide standing ground outside the system from which the system can be evaluated, critiqued, and perhaps changed. Hopeless people eventually must conform, but hope-filled people are not as dependent . . ."

In a day when demented people kill by the dozens, when we learn that nearly one-fourth of our Desert Storm casualties were the result of fire from our side, and the world's little people seem to have a different system of justice afforded them than do the rich, and when we know that God's majestic good news is entrusted to be fragile faithfulness, there has to be a special provision for hope, else life is indeed a planet of fools. Without God, people become calloused and hard.

Such new commitment is necessary and such new vision of the possible is required. Again, the Christian faith is most of all a movement, a current, a tide of deliverance to solid footing.

Called to Be Healers

This piece is being written following a leave-taking party that separated me from my gall bladder and appendix. While such an experience is not the most festive occasion I can think of, I am grateful that the days in the hospital numbered only five. I'm up to one hour of walking daily ten days after the surgery, and am convinced that more healing takes place accompanied by reasonable activity than would be the case if I gave in to the possibility of staying comfortable, which I doubt would be the case anyway.

Regardless, it causes me to wonder if healing of other kinds takes place more readily if we work through it than if we merely try to stay comfortable. Take the church, for instance. It seems to me that much of the time we try to acquire health by complaining about what is wrong, or fussing at one another about the pain that is being caused as the church is encouraged to move ahead.

In my case, with my gall bladder, there was a problem. A combination of forces and people brought treatment to the occasion. The healing presence of an assuring God, skilled doctors and their team, the prayers of many people, all combined to form a community of wholeness and renewal so far as my predicament was concerned. At the same time, I have tried to give nature all of the opportunity I can.

Here is what has been going through my mind: I thank God that my gall bladder was considered more of an issue and that someone saw that a person was involved. Much of the world's ills could be turned into creative healing if clusters of skill, grace, faith, and caring could be focused on the human situation. We grow so accustomed to seeing the world's imperfections as issues when, in reality, we should be thinking about the well-being of people. Human rights, nuclear danger, hunger, terrorism, homosexuality, Equal Rights Amendment, capital punishment, and most other divisive subjects must someday stop being mere issues and be seen in the stark reality of being human predicaments, of relating to the experiences of people.

Our society is still not healed. Probably it never will be healed to the extent that God or we would like. But there are people in our community, in Arkansas, and the whole world who are more than issues.

They are living souls in need of healing teams who will bring skill, care, and hope to them and their kind, whatever their situation may be.

The church is not something to complain about or to be exclusive about. It is not a budget; it is not a program. It is a hammer, shovel, scalpel, and medicine with which to treat humanity as human beings that are loved by Christ. They are loved in that way whether or not we know it or like it. Let us make our local church, our United Methodist Church, a healing team that lets people know we care. So many would love to see a church that can say, "Rise and walk and be whole."

Mortality and Immortality

They tell me I have to have surgery again. I don't have time for it. There are dozens of commitments, appointments in the office, the Cabinet appointment process, a special session of the Kansas East Conference, a couple of general church responsibilities, and the stuff that comes in everyday that I am not going to be able to care for. I just don't have time for absence.

But I have to do it. Somehow I have to accept what I cannot change, though it affects other people, congregations, and situations. I think the most difficult part is telling everybody in every place I'm supposed to be in the next few weeks that I can't be there.

My mind tells me that the world can get along nicely without my being there and doing what I am supposed to be and do. But my heart says, "You are surely going to mess things up." Religions have been formed out of the reality of guilt, I guess, but somehow I don't feel I'm helping religion much. I hope I have enough to keep from running on empty; I do and I will. Grace provided that. It is not self-produced.

Maybe one's usefulness is placed in better balance by an awareness of one's mortality as well as immortality. Anyway, I am already aware that a lot of strife is over small stuff; the stuff that separates instead of unites. More of us have more words that heal than we ever use. We expend more energy on junk issues than we have days to waste.

I am going to try to learn something from this. If there is any-thing worth sharing, I will probably mention it in another column. (see below)

Perceiving a New Thing

> *Remember not the former things;*
> *nor consider the things of old.*
> *Behold I am doing a new thing;*
> *now it springs forth, do you not perceive it?*
> *Isaiah 43:18–19A*

Yes, I am doing lots of perceiving these days. O, I have a lot reflecting, praying and resolving to do, but after the last couple of weeks I am working on "the new thing" that God is doing and wants me to perceive.

I came through the surgery fine. They did some biopsy work ahead of time that I didn't take as seriously as the doctors did. The tumor was larger than first observed in the pictures. It was in a difficult place. And had it not been benign, in that location, I would have been in real trouble. But it was benign. That was my first gift!

The second gift was revealed in the removal of half of my stom-ach to get the tumor. That procedure revealed the source of the trouble for which I originally sought help. My stomach is permeated by chronic ulcer disease. So, while that is not a gift, the discovery of it made possible by the incision revealed the condition that is there. The discovery is the gift.

Now comes the "Behold, I am doing a new thing; now it springs forth, do you not perceive it?" In other words, with two doctors unknowingly giving me an exegesis on what this "new thing" is, I now have the challenge of perceiving its meaning and deciding a course of action.

The message is loud and clear. Medicine has reached its limits. If

I continue as is, I can expect bleeding to occur. I have to decide about a new thing.

The way I understand it is that there are to be no more eighteen-hour days and running to every place that is believed to be a burning bush where God is bursting out all over to give me the message. God has things for other people to hear, not just me.

This sounds easy while I am convalescing. But for two months the appointment process will have to take priority. Two hours a day is my limit until May 1. No more coffee (leaded or unleaded), no regular tea, no carbonated drinks, no fried stuff, spice, et cetera. And when subtle stresses are laid on me as a gift of advice to get me to bend, don't be surprised if I give them back unclaimed. I may have to say, "Back off, that has been decided."

By the way, I'm pleased as punch at how well the special session in Kansas East went. Bishop John Wesley Hardt was so special in his willingness to come. I appreciate his willingness to come. He reports that he was made to feel so welcome. You responded faithfully to the agenda.

One really can be replaced, you know. So what new thing does God have in mind? Who knows? I know that God is more than church. Church is more than organization. And the whole enterprise is more than the Episcopacy.

I looked Death in the eye, and Death blinked first this time.

In the meantime, five hundred cards, messages, phone calls, telegrams, food, flowers and gifts from individuals, churches, Sunday School classes and children reminded me of God's "new thing."

Since May 18 of last year when Elaine became hospitalized and throughout the following months, so many of you have been so gracious during that time and her recuperation. And now, again, we are so blessed with all your expressions of love and caring.

I thank the Cabinet and so many who have graciously accepted the messages of cancellation of my presence at events. But I have a gift or two, you see, and I am trying to get those gifts assembled to see what the "new thing" is that God wants me to perceive.

I don't know if putting it together will make me a better bishop, but I believe it will make me a better person. Maybe perceiving the relationship of the two is part of the reconstruction. Thank you for your prayers, love, and concern.

Still Healing

Yep, I'm still healing, and the wellness is returning, not rapidly, but on schedule. Alfred Lord Tennyson must have been where I have been when he wrote in *Ulysses:*

> Though much is taken, much abides; and though
> We are not now that strength which in old days
> Moved earth and heaven, that which we are, we are;
> One equal temper of heroic hearts,
> Made weak by time and fate, but strong in will
> To strive, to seek, to find, and not to yield.

CHAPTER
6

More Lessons to Be
Learned

Reaching

The higher one flies
    The greater the likelihood of sunshine.
The high-flying soul
    Is one that surmounts
    The variables of struggle;
Not to avoid the struggle
    But to continue in it
    With poise and determination.

I press on, not because it is fun,
    But it is what I am called to do.
Life is constant emergency.
Life is having no food in the house,
    But setting the table anyway;
Sitting down to an empty place
    And praying,
"We thank you, Lord, for what
    We are about to receive."
                         KWH

Someone Must

If the word is proclaimed, someone must proclaim it.
If a person should be fed, someone must make that happen.
If a wound needs binding, someone must bind it.
If a mind needs teaching, someone must teach it.
If something should happen, someone must make it happen.
Onlookers limit what God wishes to occur.
Participants make it happen.
God doesn't usually do by Himself that
    which can be done with a human partner.
That's saddening or gladdening, isn't it?
It depends on whether we do or don't.
Think about it.

                    KWH

Church Functions That Are on Target

A great many of our Sundays have to do with being present as a congregation consecrates a church facility, shiny and new, for the service of Christ and the church; or to dedicate a building after years of dedicated stewardship have finally paid for the facility, enabling the congregation to offer it to God for His service; or to help celebrate an anniversary observing the fact that a church has been in existence as a congregation for a number of years. It is always a great time and a happy experience for all who attend.

There are many beautiful church facilities in our country. We can be proud of the care that people have for their church buildings.

I have noted, however, that the church as an institution is not the important thing. Various moods prevail among the congregations. One feels a climate, a mood in a congregation. Such an attitude does not correspond to the quality of the building.

Edward Bauman in a book titled *God's Presence in My Life* hits the nail on the head by suggesting that a church should be measured around three major functions. The first of these is that the church functions around the *experience of presence*. By this, I have in mind the extent to which members of the congregation somehow feel that God's reality and nearness is a dynamic factor which makes church participation worthwhile. As one man states in Bauman's book, as a period of corporate prayer was being experienced, "I was afraid to put out my hand, lest I touch God." There are churches in which to meet is close to that kind of experience. The function of "presence" is clearly to be looked for in any church. When it is there, a congregation is caught up in something that is indeed a treasure.

A second function of the church in the book mentioned is that which revolves around the *experience of mission*. There are times when, regardless of the quality of buildings, it is evident that a congregation knows it is involved in something beyond itself and is glad such is the case. A church that finds itself engaged in understanding and affecting the world even in a small way is bound to be a special church.

A third function of the church that is suggested is the *experience of community*. Sometimes the church is the extended family of the individuals in it. This is bound to mean that the congregation is one in which there is a caring and supporting presence for all. When those who are members of a congregation experience what it is to be nourished, a fortunate church exists.

Let's take a look at our church and ask ourselves and one another, "How well are we doing in experiencing presence, mission, and community?" It might be the beginning of a revival.

What's Right with Us!

We are into a new year. I wonder what we will do with it? It might benefit all of us to take the time to decide what's right with the world, the church, and our country. My real wish for the New Year is a positive mental attitude on the part of Christian people. If we can pull that off, we can become the glue that holds a fragmented world together. If we don't capture the positive nature of our faith and put it into practice, we will deprive the world of Christian hope. There is no agency or movement that can provide hope to the extent the church can.

Such a view is illustrated in a letter from a third-century Christian named Cyprian to a friend: "This seems a cheerful world, Donatus, when I view it from this fair garden under the shadow of these vines. But if I climbed some great mountain and looked out over the wide lands, you know very well what I would see. Brigands on the high roads, pirates on the seas . . . under all roofs misery and selfishness. It is really a bad world, Donatus, an incredibly bad world. Yet in the midst of it I have found a quiet and holy people. They have discovered a joy which is a thousand times better than any pleasure . . . They are despised and persecuted, but they have overcome the world. These people, Donatus, are the Christians—and I am one of them."

What a great proclamation for this particular new year! "I am one of them." This is my privilege. It is also my responsibility.

I am glad for what the church is doing well. Arkansas United

Methodism has initiated the significant Hunger Ingathering effort that is the outstanding one in the nation. In November our fourth ingathering resulted in ecumenical action amounting to $2.5 million worth of goods and cash, with one-half million of that being United Methodist giving.

Arkansas United Methodism has initiated a ministry to prisoners and their families involving at least seventeen denominations. Churches are working together in Cooperative Parish Ministries, discovering what it means to be instruments of strength by working together.

Our two Council staffs are working as an area staff on behalf of both conferences. Many churches are reporting an increase in church school and worship attendance. The likelihood of statistical growth is on the horizon.

Our church is less than perfect, but it is a church that is concerned about the things that are happening to people. Our mistakes and shortcomings reveal a church that is trying to care effectively.

Christ is calling us to repentance. He is calling us to follow. He is calling us to great believing, and also to great action in His name. He is calling us to a biblical faith that does not stop with the Bible, but which, because of the Bible, seeks the lost and the confused with the good news of Jesus Christ as Lord and friend. Happy New Year!

Sermons and Sunday Evenings

In Ralph Waldo Emerson's journal, an entry dated October 21, 1838, states, "Edward Palmer asked me if I liked two services in a Sabbath. I told him, not very well. If the sermon was good, I wished to think of it; if it was bad, one was enough." I have a certain sympathy for pastors who have to prepare two sermons each Sunday, and sort of wonder about those who relish the idea. Maybe it's because I've always done well to come up with one passable sermon for my congregation.

It isn't that I object to preaching more than once on Sunday. We would be in a fix if somebody imposed a rule that a preacher can preach only once a Sunday. But the idea of having a morning and a night sermon, or a sermon for the formal morning service and an evangelistic sermon for Sunday night is a process of sorting cats that I don't understand.

To me the task of treating the scriptures with deference, the intellect of people with respect, and centering the meaning of God in a plot of human experience with authenticity is a challenge of no small consideration. If a pastor can come within spitting distance of accomplishing this once a week, such a servant has earned his or her mark for preaching.

Now, I'm not putting down Sunday evening activity in the church. In fact, it is a wonderful occasion for the pastor and youth to get together, or for the pastor to do some teaching or participate in a discussion enterprise that is equally worthwhile to a sermon.

Some people take to sermons like eating jello. The intake can go on and on and they are never full. Such contact with sermons has doubtful benefits. If the sermon can be designed so as to occasion mental and spiritual exchange, even if not verbal, the enterprise of preaching is worthwhile. But in such instances the preaching will surely have been preceded with preparation and prayer on the part of the preacher.

When we preach we should never underestimate the intelligence of the congregation or overestimate their knowledge. To arrive at the right balance so that the person in the pew is willing to reset the course of life on hearing a sermon is to have spent all the sermon preparation time we have on doing one well per Sunday.

To each his or her own. This goes for preachers and congregations. I certainly am for lights on in the church on Sunday night, but I think there are questions that need to be asked, insights to be exchanged in conversation, and varieties of ways that a congregation might engage the call and claim of the Master.

Confirmation: Beginning of a New Relationship

This is the season when, traditionally, confirmation classes are received into full membership in the church. The United Methodist

Church has not exercised uniformity in how confirmation is to be done, when it is to be done, or what age is to be the time when acts of confirmation are to be observed. With all of the variety indulged in, all in the name of membership training, the act of confirmation itself is one in which most pastors have experienced a lump in the throat on observing youngsters kneeling to receive the rite of confirmation. However or whenever it is done, it should be experienced as a holy moment in the life of the church.

Confirmation itself is the climax of the membership training endeavor which has begun, not ended. It is a moment of recognition that a new relationship has been entered with Christ and His church. The way this relationship is intended to be verified, though, is in relationship with others—with the world no less.

Confirmation is a process of deciding to be "firm" in living out the expectation and anticipation laid upon us in the claim that God has made on our life through Christ. The service of confirmation observed as a routine event which rates slightly above society "coming out" events is sacrilege. Too often youngsters are in confirmation classes at the insistence and decision of parents alone. Parental guidance and urging is important, but confirmation is intended to touch and draw out the capacity of the one being confirmed a decision to walk in the way of Christ.

It is also a time when the church as the community of faith should be called upon to declare its intention to be a supportive fellowship which humbly, yet joyously, receives new life into its midst, and renews its commitment as the vows of new life are expressed.

Confirmation is not so much receiving new members as it is celebration that Christ and persons have been joined in fresh intentions. The result should be newness of life in the persons who take the vows for the first time. Just as important is the recognition of the new life and responsibility that has permeated the existing congregation.

When rightly observed, the service of confirmation is experienced in the meaning of the word itself, becoming "firm with"

Christ and one another to form a new relationship with existence
itself. At the heart of it all is the recognition that a new center exists
in our behavior, the meaning of which is God.

A Tapestry of Faith

It is purported that Calvin Coolidge said, "If you don't say anything, you won't be asked to repeat it." I think he was right. At least
my mail would indicate so. In fact, I have found out that if you say
nothing controversial, you don't have to explain what you meant or
why you meant it. That's rather nice now and then, having some
noncontroversial time, that is.

Where, though, is the growing edge of faith? Isn't it in examining
the issues in the light of biblical insight? It seems to me that the
nature of the Bible is such that it continually calls the world into
question. Peace, hunger, international relations, poverty, stewardship,
and all the other arenas of human experience contain not only the
human predicament, but the God predicament as well. The adventure of living, with all the deciding, crying, and laughing inherent
in it, is the data within which the Christ agenda must be sorted out.
I used to think that the world and what is going on in it is the
agenda for the church. My mind has made a circle about that. I am
in the process of concluding that Christ is the agenda and the
human goings-on around us provide the environment in which that
agenda is confronted.

If this is true, then we don't manipulate education, human beings,
or laws so that the Bible is verified. The Bible doesn't require proof.
It requires expression in life forms so that the wonder and reality of
God continues to be revealed through our human systems, decisions,
and behavior. How this looks when strained through our evangelism
and educational efforts defines, not only our church, but also the
personal quality of Christian concern and commitment.

A university educator said, so goes the story, that the university
could be a great place if it weren't for the students. It is just as unre-
alistic to say that the church could do a great job of evangelizing and
educating to be Christian if it weren't for the nature of the world. But

this world is the fabric we have for our weaving. If our efforts are insistent that the design of our tapestry shall reveal Christ, then we have direction for our hope and a task by which to shape our dreams.

Meaning of the Symbol

Which matters most, symbol or substance? I am referring to the Cross and Flame, the symbol of our United Methodist Church. I can and have experienced other models of descriptive logo representing our church and, maybe, will again.

I like the Cross and Flame. Not that it is all that beautiful, but I like driving down the road and seeing the familiar sign with directions giving the location of the church building. I know something of the meaning of the Cross and Flame. It represents sacrifice, resurrection, as well as being a reminder that there is a Spirit we call Holy inherent in the meaning of The United Methodist Church. I know it symbolically spells evangelism, nurture, justice, and salvation.

But when I get to the building, or better yet, the congregation of which that symbol directed me, I experience the substance of the Cross and Flame. Sometimes, the substance is inspiring, moving, and life-changing. On other occasions the substance is cold, routine, and tense. It is possible that there is little connection between the substance of the symbol and the quality of life encountered in the fellowship.

I really hope the General Conference will not tinker with the symbol in my lifetime. It pleasures me to see it honored and fulfilled. It grieves me to see it discounted, desecrated, or its heritage left unexamined.

The substance of the Cross and Flame must be decided as the hearts of persons open to the flame of the Holy Spirit. Its meaning takes on quality, as people become not only a great church in numbers, but also great in quality of service and discipleship. I am proud when I see the symbol alive in a congregation that has decided to be in mission.

You can't legislate in a General or Annual Conference what the symbol will really look like. Some churches have a simple board sign giving direction to a center of spiritual power acted out in and through a congregation.

On my walk recently, I met a man removing the remains of his bashed mailbox. Some people had smashed mailboxes for two miles. He said, "I've put up several mailboxes. It isn't the box that's important, but whether or not you get the mail." The Cross and Flame sign is important, but it doesn't tell whether or not our church is "delivering the mail."

Be Substance, Not Symbol

How exciting is going to church? It seems to depend on several things, none of which are automatic to the nature of Christ's church, the universal church. A listless congregation, too lazy or too tired or too indifferent to sing, dilutes the enthusiasm.

A preacher who is tired, underprepared, or who is dedicated to saying only safe things can make it seem like we are reliving the church of thirty years ago. Ralph Waldo Emerson said in an address at Divinity College, Cambridge, Massachusetts, in 1938 that he once heard a preacher who sorely tempted him to say he would go to church no more.

What was the issue with Emerson? He said of the preacher, "This man had ploughed and planted and talked and bought and sold; he had read books; he had eaten and drunken; his head aches, the heart throbs; he smiles and suffers yet there was not a surmise, a hint, in all the discourse, that he had ever lived at all."

Sometimes the Gospel, as encased in the church, is like a memory encased in an institution. It is treated as something of a relic.

How long has it been since you heard even a United Methodist politician ask, "What does our church think about this?" Most of the time political figures don't care what the church thinks or teaches because the consequences the church can produce aren't that heavy.

Do you see, or do you contribute to, an enthusiasm about the engagement of the church in mission? We might assess what are the energy points in our congregation that would attract and hold the companionship of those who come our way. I have a quotation from Sam Shoemaker which says, "Act as if the whole thing, the Gospel, the Good News, the reality and love of God as revealed by Christ—act as if it were all true. Behave as if you believed." Jesus said, "As you think in your heart, so are you."

There are many traumatic components in the daily encounters of people and nations. In the midst of the mix, there is ample evidence of the need for the Christian people to consider whether the church or any congregation can afford to be a symbol of righteousness or, on the other hand, whether we must recognize that it is a substance intended to be salt and yeast in the affairs of God and humanity. If the latter is true, we had better get cracking!

I have been doing some special summer reading of scripture, especially Luke and Acts, two books of the Bible which probably share the same author. A feature that seizes my attention is that the Gospel of Luke describes an activist teacher, Jesus describing with the help of a large cast, a pro-people stance as He proclaims his Gospel. Luke gives us a heavy dose of substance.

Acts describes the formation of the church as it encounters principalities and powers. It is spirit-filled substance that changes people and a structure, the church, that continues the incarnation event in form.

Form (the church) followed Substance (the risen Christ). The structure of the world shook under the impact. It is such a time for such an experience again. I call that real evangelism. Isn't that worth considering?

Atlanta Airport

America, yes, even the world passes by where I sit.
Funny hats from a tour someplace;
Someone trying to steer Grandma into the boarding pass line.
There is one with jacket and straw hat.
Someone's meeting another someone getting assistance from a
cane.
"Go to Gate 17." "Take a right to the transportation area."
"Hi, sweetie. I'm fine; how about yourself?"
There's one who knows exactly what he wants to do and can't.
A man with a ceramic pot.
A woman with no bra.
One with nothing for a bra.
A poet type, frail, pale, bearded—135 pounds
      and a pipe that holds a packet of tobacco.
Humanity passes before me.

Even more does it pass before God, here in this
      microcosm of the world.
And God seems to say, "Settle down and know that the universe
      needs you at your best.
Love when you can.
      Forgive when you can.
I would that you might know that every ounce of divinity
      expressed through a human being is an impact for eternity."

God said to me, "I long to see expressions of incarnations, for
      that is my intention.
I am limited just by being God, but humans—
my sons and daughters—have so much to offer.

That indeed is my plan;
    that the shepherd, the fishermen, poets, the laborers
    of the world will witness to my greatest desire—
      to incarnate myself in human form.
Ah! That will save my world!"

So, let us run, let us sift out chaff.
Let us believe only to incarnate the rhythm and spirit
    of the one who has so much grace to give.

As I left to board my flight, God said a word to all.
I happened to catch its whisper, enough to know
    that though it was a word to all,
I had heard, so I must be claimed by it, as must
    each one who hears the whisper:
"Be saved by letting yourself be formed.
    Be eternal by dying to self.
      Be your best by letting me become your center."
           KWH

Editor's note: The following two entries are favorite writings of Bishop Hicks that he has treasured for years.

What Is Class?

Class never runs scared. It is sure-footed and confident in the knowledge that you can meet life head on and handle whatever comes along.

Jacob had it. Esau didn't. Symbolically, we can look to Jacob's wrestling match with the angel. Those who have class have wrestled with their own personal angel and won a victory that marks them thereafter.

Class never makes excuses. It takes its lumps and learns from past mistakes.

Class is considerate of others. It knows that good manners are nothing more than a series of small sacrifices.

Class bespeaks an aristocracy that has nothing to do with ancestors or money. The most affluent blueblood can be totally without class while the descendant of a Welsh miner may ooze class from every pore.

Class never tries to build itself up by tearing others down. Class is already up and needs not strive to look better by making others look worse.

Class can "walk with kings and keep its virtue and talk with crowds and keep the common touch." Everyone is comfortable with the person who has class because he is comfortable with himself.

If you have class, you don't need much of anything else. If you don't have it, no matter what else you have, it doesn't make much difference.

Ann Landers Encyclopedia

The moral test of government is how it treats
those who are in the dawn of life, the children;
those who are in the twilight of life, the aged;
and those who are in the shadows of life
—the sick, the needy and the handicapped.

                    Sen. Hubert H. Humphrey

CHAPTER

7

Peace with Justice

Give Back to God

I wish for all whom I know and love
A peace of heart that tells them
They are accepted;
And, that they can accept life—
Accept it, receive it, absorb it,
give it back to God.
The worst—or the best that life can give is your gift.
If suffering, then suffer and offer it to God as your gift.
If sorrow, then be sorrowful, and offer it to God as your gift.
If joy, then be joyful and give it to God.
For in such giving you give who you are, what you are.
God receives it as you. It is what you are.
It is what you were given to be and to use.

Nothing else can be given to God.

So, don't wait until you can give saintliness.
Don't wait until you can give perfection.
Give him what you have experienced, for that is who you are.
Give that, and that is enough to make
a new birth and a resurrection.

                              KWH

Peace Is More Than the Absence of War

Peace with Justice provides a special cutting edge of meaning that
penetrates the relationships in which people are engaged and their
decisions about those relationships.

To put it another way, Peace with Justice is not a program to push,
but a life to encounter. It is discipleship with a concern for people,
the components that comprise their life, and the preservation of the
world God has given us to use. It is His, not ours . . .

We must surrender as obsolete the process of thinking of peace
as the absence of war. Peace with Justice is not the intervals between
wars. Peace with Justice is linkage with transformation, rebirth,
reconciliation—not just of personal lives—but of systems, relationships, economics, family, lifestyle, human rights. The dangers *and*
the opportunities are so numerous and so great on the world scene
that peace must infiltrate every decision we make about each other
everywhere.

Peace with Justice calls for study of scripture, not just for what the
Bible says, but with regard to what it means. Peace with Justice sees
salvation, not just in the private sense, but as all of humanity in
covenant . . . this means the mandate of corporate dimensions of conversion (and) what it means to be part of a Christian congregation.

Peace with Justice assumes a stance that looks at the totality of
human experience as it is and as God wants it to be. The future is
precarious enough that peace must be seen in a broader sense than
the absence of conflict . . .

The peace we strive for in this special program launches us into
an agenda of salvation, hope, liberation, wholeness, and justice itself
. . . The Hebrew word that gathers all of this into a lifestyle is
"Shalom."

Biblical peace engages more than militaristic solutions. It commands us to drive to the centers of potential outcome, those new
centers of experience at which decisions are made about values,
attitudes, and qualities of relationships. All of this, in accordance with
"Shalom," must be penetrated and confronted by God's spirit and
desire. A new heaven and a new earth is the vision of John's "Rev-

elation"—not one that is in a holding pattern, or a creation of a temporary committee that designed a mixture of conflict and armistice—but a new creation.

Peace with Justice is a life of reconciliation as a mandate from God, given to us through Christ as our ministry, the objective of which is to reconcile the world to himself. For the Christian it is not a call to be decent, but to be in mission.

"PWJ"

Isaiah 11 says, "There shall come forth a shoot from the stump of Jesse, and a branch shall grow out of his roots. And the Spirit of the Lord shall rest upon him . . ." A bit further into the chapter there are words about this anticipated one who will judge with righteousness rather than by what his eyes see.

Then, as a result of his faithfulness, "The wolf shall dwell with the lamb, and the leopard shall lie down with the kid, and the calf and the lion and the fatling together, and a little child shall lead them."

We sometimes read into this our own image of a picture of utopia. It occurs to me that Isaiah is describing PWJ. Instead of three letters he uses verbal exaggeration to suggest that God is really serious to the point of being radically descriptive. The righteousness and faithfulness that result in peace calls for a reordering of leadership images ("a little child shall lead them"). It is intended that new manifestations in relationships shall be experienced ("the leopard shall lie down with the goat").

Is it possible that the way to peace is not the way of the bomb and the missile? Where are the aggressive images toward peace that are as bold as the images toward war? What is God meaning to say in this radical scripture in Isaiah 11? There are fascinating words in this reference for consideration by the church. "Righteousness," "judge," "poor," "faithfulness"—all are words culminating in a revamped existence. Passages such as Isaiah 11 could be troublesome to some of us, unless we sentimentalize the seriousness of God about our plight right out of the picture. I have a hunch the Lord and Isaiah will win out. They had better!

Mailgram

3/15/85

This is a confirmation copy of the following message:

9132720587 MGMB TDBN Topeka KS 47 03-15 0242P EST

Zip

Senator Nancy Kassebaum

United States Senate

Washington DC 20510

Dear Senator Kassebaum

I have just learned that you are opposing the MX. Thank you for your stand for a halt to the arms madness. God bless you.

Sincerely

Kenneth W Hicks, Bishop Kansas Area United Methodist Church

Plowshares and Peacemakers

We do not seek health by trying to become sick. We do not build a savings account by spending all our money. Why do we think we can have Peace with Justice by heavy emphasis on war and the instruments of war?

The word from Isaiah concerning beating swords into plowshares and Jesus' beatitude, "Blessed are the peace *makers,*" imply that lasting peace is attained through a radical change of life's values and styles.

It may be that the prospects for peace are dim because our efforts for peace are shallow and few compared to the preparations we make for war. "Swords into plowshares" implies a replacement of values. "Peacemakers" is a term denoting aggressive compassion for turning things around.

Poverty, oppression, sickness, unemployment, and the absence of Christian values all contain the roots of war. Peace with Justice implores us to deal with the roots of war.

Who can do this with greater spiritual authority than the church?

Ultimately, of course, these matters must have the attention of law-makers, designers of social services, and others who formulate the structures that affect humanity.

We stand in the unique position in America of being in the position to challenge the whole world, including our adversaries to accept a new premise for peace, one that goes beyond preparing for war in the hopes it will not be needed. We have the reservoir of a faith and a gospel and a Christ. Christians should offer more by way of insight that will make the prophetic word and the blessing of Jesus on peacemakers a reality.

"What If We Give a War and Nobody Shows Up?"

This is a "what if" column. A "what if" list isn't practical in the sense of being likely to happen. It's just an exercise in wondering what things would be like given a different way of doing things.

What if a law were to be passed declaring that in case of war those over fifty would be the first to go? Would as many wars be started?

What if the United Nations were to lease some place, say the Falkland Islands, to be the place where, if two nations want to fight, they would go there to do it? All wars would be held there.

What if, when war is declared no one shows up to fight it? What's a war if nobody shows up?

What if, instead of nuclear bombs and missiles that become constantly outmoded, each nation had one super man who had been bombarded with vitamins, weightlifting, muscle building, hormones, and whatever else makes a man macho and strong; then when there is a war, just those single adversaries were put in an arena to represent their nation just one-on-one? Or better yet, what if each soldier were provided a good stick with a limit in length, say of five or six feet? The outcome could still be decided, but the decisive outcome would omit the billions of dollars now spent on armaments.

What if wars were resolved by having maybe ten adversaries on each side who would make faces at the other side? They could have spent months in training to stretch their faces in grotesque shapes.

An international body of judges would decide which side made the best "uglies" at the other side.

What if, instead of computerized tanks costing millions of dollars each, the warring nations staged a demolition derby? They could even use new cars. Think of the jobs it would provide the auto builders at much less cost. Tickets could be sold, and military cheerleaders could be provided. Maybe hats and flags could be side concessions that would make the whole thing paid for by the time it was over.

What if an international law existed that says the members of the legislative bodies who decide to have a war will engage one another in the first skirmish?

What if the commandment "thou shalt not kill" were taken as seriously as the passages on sexuality: or if "love thy neighbor" were taken as literally as "wives, obey your husbands?"

What if, with regard to justice, we really believed that when we help the oppressed, the naked, the hungry, we would really be doing it for Christ?

What if we knew that unless we do, we are done for?

Peace with Justice Restated

It is clear that peace and justice are tied together. In a day when technology is so visible, even to peasants, nomads, and the hungry; when electronic media carry the news of the world to the most remote places on earth; it is natural that there is a stirring and a restlessness for security and for the possession of basic necessities.

To "beat swords into plowshares" is to replace wooden plows for steel ones. It is to replace the danger of being displaced from a patch of ground called home for the privilege of calling one's dwelling place one's own. A seedbed for war and revolution abide when these dreams are not possible.

So *Peace with Justice* endeavors to involve the church in efforts to change priorities as a result of theological commitment, so that we begin our critical gaze on the world by seeing people everywhere as those created by God. The real enemy is war, not people.

Jesus *Is* Peace

An article by Thomas Merton has helped me as I attempt to bring a word of hope. Thomas Merton was a Trappist monk. He notes that peace may mean the liberty to exploit people without fear of interference. For another, it may mean the leisure to devour the goods of the earth without being compelled to be considerate of those who are starving. Still another may feel that peace is simply the absence of violence.

He suggests that if our prayers for peace emerge from those attitudes, our prayers may indeed be answered as God leaves us with what we desire. Such defective notions of peace are simply other forms of war.

Our friend, Merton, proposes that instead of loving what we think is peace we should love other people and love God above all. And instead of hating the people we think are war makers, hate the appetites and the disorder in our own soul which are the causes of war.

Another thought might be added. Jesus does not merely point the way toward peace. Jesus *is* peace. To call ourselves His disciples is to commit ourselves to peace itself for peace is what Jesus is. We Christians struggle with Jesus' teachings about peace, when the real struggle is what to do with Jesus who is peace—the Prince of Peace.

This puts in the forefront the question: Can a nation profess Jesus and resort to war at the same time, or is there something radical about following Jesus who is Peace Incarnate?

For a Christian, if we love peace, then we oppose injustice, tyranny, greed—but we must hate them in ourselves, not just in others. The Christ in us and in the church is the real issue in Peace versus War.

So the war our country faces is a spiritual issue, not just a military one. We must pray for all who are suffering and in danger. We must support our own personnel by praying for their return soon.

In the meantime, along with prayer, it is okay to question, to reason and to ask questions of our methodology for resolving conflict. Those, too, are supportive actions.

Peace, Ready or Not?

Isaiah has a positive word for us in chapter 60, verses 17 and 18. Some of his lines from God include these: "I will appoint Peace as your overseer and Righteousness as your taskmaster. Violence shall no more be heard in your land ... you shall call your walls Salvation, and your gates Praise."

Now, as I understand words like these I think God is posing a new vocabulary for living the life of hope. God has the gifts—call them alternative weapons if you wish—but God doesn't impose them. To have such assurance folks have to believe that Peace is stronger than war. Righteousness as a taskmaster is stronger than violence. Salvation and Praise are more revolutionary than politics. But God cannot give what people aren't prepared to receive.

Faith comes at the point or to the degree that we are ready to test out the validity of God's promise. So far, even organized religion is not presenting an outcry of objection to the methodology in place.

Could we be at a point in history when God's people might rise up and say to the politicians of the world, "War is no longer viable. We elected you to be statespersons. Are you up to it or not?"

No More "Church as Usual"

Do I have a book for you? *The Fate of the Earth* by Jonathan Schell is such a book. It is a book about the danger of nuclear holocaust. In addition to being a book that presents a description of the horrible reality of nuclear war, it is also about the meaning of life in such a world. He speaks of life and death, love and fear with passion and nobleness of thought.

You won't find it difficult to read, but you will have to make some decisions as to where you stand.

This brings me to an insight I carried away from our last Council of Bishops meeting. It is that church work and Christian living, which conducts itself as it has in the past, is out of touch with the world in which God has given us a parcel of time to live out. "Church" as usual is no longer "Church." The hardest decisions responsible nations have ever made are before us. Equipping our people to think "God" is to take into account His world, His treasure, His poor, His claim. Schell offers this conclusion: "In no saying of His did Christ ever suggest that the two great commandments—to love God and to love one's neighbor—could in any way be separated, or that the former could be used as a justification for violating the latter."

Faith Con Carne

In a previous article I tried to describe the importance of us carrying into the new year the value of "being" and not just "doing." Translating that concern into terms that would contribute to the "world family" is, to my thinking, the challenge of the age. In a mailing from an organization called Institute for World Order I note that the human predicament includes the following:

450 million people suffer from hunger or malnutrition
870 million adults can not read or write
12 million babies die every year before their first birthday
2 *billion* people do not have safe water to drink

The article goes on to say that the world spends 2,300 times more for military activities than it does for peacekeeping. This is impressive in a negative sort of way.

Who am I? Who are we? Where does my responsibility begin and end? Where do any of us draw the line and say, "these are included in my concern while those are excluded?" Are not those included in the statistics above part of us and ours? If not, then who is "us" and who are "ours"?

By being a child of God I am a child of the world because the world and those in it are His. The Kingdom of God surely is not limited to the borders of the United States or to United Methodists. Nor is it limited to the unborn when 12 million newborn do not see their second year.

Where shall our emphasis be placed? There is only one answer I think: on the totality of life, its wholeness. As Wesley said, "The world is my parish." There is an inclusiveness in such an insight that won't let us be smug or self-assured. No longer can we make our offering in the temple and carry away salvation in a package. Part of our hope for the world is withheld until all have hope. We are surely challenged with the possibility that we can only receive the peace and assurance we are willing to give. It is a paradox of faith that we receive what we need by giving it. Put in the language of love and caring, the result is peace with justice. Or, to say it another way, faith con carne (faith with flesh around it).

Violence Is Like Pancakes

The increase in the reality of violence in our society is at the point at which one must acknowledge it to be the social climate of our day. Violence is not only the response of the unlawful. It permeates the minds of the good, even of our leaders.

Violence is like pancakes. You put one on top of the other. One violent act begets another. The higher the stack of pancakes, the more syrup is required to make the whole mess palatable.

Is there a statesman, a theologian, or a philosopher, perhaps an ordinary citizen, who can think of the future in terms of ideas and values that are alternative solutions to violence? We have emasculated the word "peace" in political circles by making the word synonymous with greater firepower than the enemy has. We have simplified who the enemy is by labels, when both the feared and fearful in this potential holocaust rest in our own unwillingness or inability to really think and live our peace.

So, in current official circles, the way to peace is to prepare for war. The way to solve criminal acts of violence is to retaliate by leg-

islated acts of violence. It is suggested that executions should be tel-
evised, which is a small step from frontier practices of full Main
Streets on hanging days.

Have we come so little distance? Is the best that civilized people
can come up with merely the moving of the crime of the lawless
to a realm of vengeance by the lawful? Again, that repetitive stacking
of the pancakes requires abundant syrup of justification. Ultimately
the digestive system of humanity's innards can stand only so much
dietary imbalance.

As to war, its conventional shape as an alternative to nuclear war
cannot be justified. In the last three years, according to columnist
James Reston, six new wars have started with more than 4 million
people engaged in combat. The civilian toll cannot be determined
except that conventional war now kills more civilians than ever
before.

The United States and the Soviet Union are the major suppliers
of military arms to the world. There is a great deal of talk about
world interdependence but little creative conversation, to say nothing of action, about the causes of world violence.

The sanctity of life is hardly talked about in government circles
except when it is around the issue of abortion. Human rights are
discussed not with reference to human beings but with reference to
political entities; often it is related to shoring up oppressive governments in the interest of economics.

Archibald MacLeish has said, "We are the best informed people
on earth. We are deluged with facts, but we have lost or are losing
our human ability to feel them . . . I know only that this impotence
exists and that it is dangerous—increasingly dangerous."

Dr. Karl Menninger said recently that the aggressive nature of
Americans and their unwillingness to pursue peace inevitably means
self-destruction. "We are a violent, belligerent, aggressive people
. . . Too many people in American society are so confused and preoccupied with either dominating others or the fear of being dom-
inated that they do not know how to deal with problems civilly.
Aggression results in self-destruction."

When one looks at the life of Jesus, our prevailing style does not mesh with His. When the woman taken in adultery was about to be stoned by the established religious standards of the day, He turned the attention from the one assessed to be the criminal to those who were about to take violent reprisal and asked them to examine themselves, their own values and behavior.

I don't think Jesus was standing on the side of crime, but was asking that society evaluate itself as to its values, morals, and self-righteousness. Does violent retaliation undo the crime? Does it bring back the victim? Or is it simply a release of vengeance and an outlet for society's anger?

One thing is clear, civil people who are righteously motivated seem to move through their days in the certain knowledge that the outcome is God's. History belongs to God. The earth is the Lord's. If this be true then we must beware lest we allow ourselves to assume the role of God as if there is no sin in us.

I do not see at the present moment a world becoming more civilized. I do not see religion being the cohesive, peacemaking shaper of human events it has the opportunity to be or that it is called to be.

When humaneness is branded as bleeding heart liberalism, when peacemaking is to be labeled subversive, when withholding of church contributions becomes the stewardship strategy of the church, when ecumenical social witness is condemned, then we must look into our soul to see if we are being motivated by the fullness of God's grace and love or by an emptiness we call God.

However much we may justify the labels we put on nations, groups of individuals, or persons of whom we disapprove, let us know that some sudden disappearance of these so labeled still requires us to examine the sin in ourselves. The boycotting and neglect of the potential capacity each of us has to redeem some small piece of earth and its people is a part of us that needs the remedy of a Christlike God. The tendency toward allowing or encouraging judgment to prevail over grace must be dealt with through study, prayer, and reason. This route, it seems to me, is the way to God's intention.

The Defense Budget and Me

The way I look at it as a clergyperson and Christian, it is not my role to defend the defense budget. It is not my role to defend the Pentagon. I don't have to defend the State Department. They have lobbyists by the hundreds and hundreds that are taking care of their interest, but I have responsibility as a Christian to advocate for the role or place of love, reconciliation, and understanding and forgiveness and all those characteristics of our Christian Gospel. Nobody is going to advocate for those values if we don't do it ... I am willing to throw my efforts and influence at the point at which I do feel a responsibility and a calling. I'm not saying that the United States shouldn't have—indeed, I can't imagine that we would ever not have—an armed forces whatsoever. But, it is an imperative to constantly call into question the intention and the ability to create the annihilation of the human race. I think there has to be somebody who constantly resists that, even to the point of denouncing it. Otherwise, human values and spiritual values are not going to be advocated. People sometimes say, "You would have us just lay down our arms, disband all of our nuclear testing?" That is not what I am saying. That is an area that it is very obvious will be taken care of. But who speaks for peace? Therefore we must do it. We hope that out of that tension, not disloyalty, will come the creative cauldron out of which a lasting humanity could occur.

The Criminal Justice System

I would like to say that I do not consider myself an expert on the criminal justice system. Still, even from that standpoint, I feel that there are an awful lot of gaps in the justice system, in terms of consistency of equal treatment of all people. The poor, the disadvantaged people, the elderly, and even children—these are the people who probably have much less choice in the total justice system than the middle-to-upper-class person who has the economic clout to buy appropriate legal representation.

There is no doubt that there is an inequality of justice and it is

simply because there is not an equality of resources and advocates
for certain categories of people. That is part of the problem we face
with our system now.

I think it is debatable as to whether the harshest kinds of punishment ever really did work. Looking at the level of violence we have
in our society today, it would not seem that the most physical and
punitive kinds of justice have made a whole lot of improvements
toward the reign of goodness and kindness. I think we do turn, and
have turned, some people loose before they have been appropriately
punished or rehabilitated. Many times this depends again upon the
extent to which the person has the resources to acquire the legal
clout—to get early parole, sentences modified, and that sort of
action.

Refugees from the South

Some folk die in the sand of the desert.
Human refugees trying to find life
It is said they should have had five gallons of water.
Even this was not their possession.

Some make it—some don't.

I ask, "Who in Kansas or Nebraska knows?"
Who cares?
Why did they leave their habitat anyway?
Who hears the answer, "We look for sustenance
for those we have left and for ourselves?"

Who will make the government human?
Can the conscience of politics override the
thirst for votes?

What is a human worth?
For some lives there is no market.
But we still have to decide, don't we?

Life is carelessly taken not only by gangsters.
We take it in a thousand ways,
not by a knife
or a gun,
But by a vote; by not caring;
or by allowing it to happen.
                    KWH

Opposition to the Death Penalty

Editor's note: The following is an excerpt from the front page
article of the February 3, 1989, issue of the United Methodist
Review published by the Kansas West Annual Conference.

Bishop Hicks has long been a vocal opponent of capital punishment. He was among those testifying against the proposals to rein-
state it considered by the 1987 Kansas Legislature.

He says there is no evidence the threat of execution is a deterrent
to criminals.

Even if it could be proved to be a deterrent, he continues, "I
would still be against it. My theology believes a part of God's image
is in every person. To destroy a human being, no matter how good
or evil, is really a destruction of a part of God's creation."

With no evidence of it being a deterrent, he says, "That leaves the
only reason for the death penalty to be saying we want to rid ourselves of the perpetrator of the crime. It is a means of institutional-
izing and legalizing violence which there's enough of already
without legalizing it."

Imposing the death penalty "doesn't bring back the one or ones
whose lives have been taken," the bishop adds, "but it allows society
to enter into the same sort of disgusting behavior done on the first
victim." He notes Kansas "has a lower homicide rate per 1000
people than do most states that have the death penalty."

Besides stating his basic opposition to capital punishment, Bishop
Hicks cites justice issues surrounding imposition of the death
penalty.

"It is not an equitable penalty," he says. "People of color and poor
people are disadvantaged in such a situation because of the lack of
resources to carry them through the appeal system. The data seems
to show the people who can afford private legal counsel fare better
than those found guilty of some form of murder who have to rely
on the public system. The reality is that the poor people are the ones
who are executed disproportionately."

He also points out people have been executed who were later found to be innocent. "There is no possible way of correcting the error after the person's life is gone."

Bishop Hicks' opposition to capital punishment mirrors the official United Methodist position on the issue.

A New World Order

A New World Order will emerge one day, and it should declare itself through the expressed convictions of people declaring that war is old-fashioned. Don't dress-up war in clothing implying newness of human relationships!

As the New World Order stands, we find an already staggering debt bending under the burden of a billion dollars a day. That is going to impact the world of my grandchildren.

The existing New World Order is decimating the fabric of family to the extent that family scars for at least a generation or longer will exist as a result of the separations being required in our households. This is not a pro-family stance.

The New World Order is assessing my grandchildren with a future citizen debt load that will overload the economy to the point that can't be fathomed.

The *real* New World Order may require a time when the people take charge of government again and say, *"War is unacceptable." "It is of the Stone Age." "If you wish to lead us, care about us, and if you wish to lead us and form political policy, we think the time is here for leadership to learn how to empower statesmanship. If you won't, then get out of the way, for the future belongs to those who will learn of the skills of peace aggression not military aggression, and who will really rise to the challenge of a new order of diplomacy, and international relations."*

We must say to the future, "You will no longer take our loved ones and ask them to give their lives for such nebulous and dimly designed ends."

Now, I'm not proposing isolationism. That, too, is impossible in the shrinking of the global reality. I am proposing a global community in which *peace becomes a force not a weakness.* The United Nations cannot be used only when it suits our interests to do so. Neither can the World Court. This makes international deliberation bodies a mockery.

America is a *powerful* nation. We have yet to see the extent to which we can become a *great* nation.

War kills. War pollutes. War impoverishes. War kills the young and the old. War is racist. War heightens distrust in the international community. War destroys—does not BUILD. War hates—and does not LOVE. War wounds—and does not HEAL.

War cannot be measured in tanks or planes deployed and expended. War can only be measured in tears, sadness, scars, and bitterness.

Goodness must come to this globe whose people are thrust together in dependency and geography. No nation is so well equipped to exhibit goodness as we are, but unless the people have a vision of their innate goodness, they perish.

I will tell you this. After this is over I never want to hear a politician or a street citizen for that matter say, "(Oh yes) we need to assist the homeless. We need to address abuse of drugs and family members. Indeed there are so many poor. It's a shame so many children are living in poverty. But we just don't have the resources."

We have proved that to be a lie. We have proven in this debacle that we have funding for what is expedient. *If war is where our heart is then we have money for it,* obviously we do. It doesn't take us long to make appropriate speeches to go to war. We can make arrangements in a matter of weeks to spend toward a billion dollars a day for war.

But how long does it take to open the door to childcare that matters; to poverty solutions that matter; to civil rights laws that make a difference.

New World Order? No, my friends this isn't it. We must turn to the old words about turning swords into plowshares and spears into pruning hooks of which Isaiah spoke. I realize that is radical, but Isaiah said it, I didn't. When you have turned swords and spears into plows and pruning hooks, you don't have swords and spears anymore. Now that's a NEW ORDER—GOD'S NEW ORDER.

Let us love all people and pray for those who are suffering the ravages of war. Let us love our loved ones enough to claim the *REAL* New Order—God's Order. Let us support our people on the front lines enough to be prepared to receive them back never to allow this again.

CHAPTER
8

Bishop Business,
Part II

During General Conference, 1988

What are the dogs doing today?
Are they up by the water tower?
I dare say they must be tromping somewhere
      if it is a cool day.
I hear my shoes on the gravel.
I hear Bandit bidding the others to come.
The sky is always beautiful where they are.
They love to lie in the ditchwater.
I would like to be down by the creek
      watching the dogs take their swim,
      wade in the backwater of the lake,
      come up smiling to the road,
      meet Ninja.
Off toward home we would go.
Old Brown Dog is more trusting all
      the time.
Poor creature, nearly blind, trotting
      gingerly.
Each step done safely is a happy piece
      of the journey for him.
I wish I were there instead of here.
                     KWH

In a Meeting of Bishops

The electricity of tedium is like
    a burnt out light bulb which we have
    been clicking, clicking to get a response,
    but it doesn't work.
Darkness—and over-elasticized interest
    muscles have given out.
Faces speak words which we are told they
    can be located in written form,
as if seeing the words would be to discover
    embers more interesting than the ashes of
    the words to which I am listening.
O Lord, how deep is the tide of the prosaic
    through which I wade just now.
The spokesman said he is about to conclude.
I didn't know he had begun.
I finished this meeting before I came
    this afternoon.
How can we do that which we cannot describe?
That seems to be the issue the verbal
    wrestling is emoting around.
                    KWH

Keeping Priorities Straight

Sometimes life gets so filled with junk to the extent that one has to start checking off some things which one judges are not worth getting upset about. I find that even when I have a full schedule and a plentiful agenda carrying life along in a normal fashion, along comes stuff that tries to get me sidetracked. And fortunately, after varying degrees and moments of distraction, I get righted back and focused again toward the intended direction. And many times that restoration comes about because of you.

As I visit local churches throughout Arkansas, I am reinforced in the value of our United Methodist heritage. We have been and are now a noble church having proclaimed Christ through witness and service for over two hundred years; and I want to get on with it.

Throughout the world there are the unchurched and the unrelated all around us. The danger of war is daily. Each day 12,000 children die before their first birthday because of malnutrition and neglect.

Every Annual Conference has a Philander Smith College, a Hendrix College, a Camp Aldersgate, or a prison ministry literally crying for enthusiastic support by Christians who want to get the job done. We have Sunday School classes to maintain, the grief-stricken to comfort, the Word to proclaim, and hymns to sing.

Let's work together to see what the meaning of being a Christian is in a world that is un-Christian, yet what the power of the Gospel is in a world that is a global community. Let us remake the soul of our time for the sake of Christ. Where there is error, correct it. Where there is injustice, change it; and where there is sin, transform it.

I know I have work to do and so do all of us who are serious about discipleship. And therein we are followers of Christ.

A Prayer for Peace

This past week I had the privilege of joining with other religious leaders in visits to our senators and one of our representatives during their late summer recess at home. Our purpose was to share with these political figures what we are feeling and experiencing regarding our assessments of the human predicament, and to encourage them in our areas of mutual concern.

There was not unanimity of course. It was good, however, to be able to lay our concerns before those who are participants in lawmaking, and to hear their views as well.

Reflection dictates the opinion that there is an uneasiness that is no less than uncertainty as to how to get hold of the problems of a society as complex as ours. The dynamics of political "how to do it" are multiple.

Do human beings have priority so that government and the free enterprise systems become expressions of the common good? Or do we believe that our structures—political and economic—become good so that people will ultimately benefit as resources move down through the systems to the people? There is probably something of both to be desired. And yet, the outcome may not be the same. It appears to this observer that the prevailing model is that which is related to the second question above. Oversimplified, this position would say that growth and consumption make jobs rather than that jobs create the development desired or that arms make peace rather than people make peace.

Somehow I get the idea that with the strengthening of everything toward "bigness" and "more" at the top, it is assumed that things and people who are small will eventually receive their just share.

I've been reading things in the Bible about swords and plowshares, big barns and mustard seeds, the mighty versus becoming as little children. There are times when the scriptures comfort. There are times when they disturb. At this writing I find myself in the disturbed crowd; but in faith mind you—faith enough to pray:

Come Holy Presence
Come as fire that burns and purges all that is
    unChristlike.
Come as rain that brings the life of heaven to earth,
    giving nourishment and growth.

Come as wind that refreshes and comforts when the way is hard.
Come as the sun whose warmth and quiet power brings
      light and power to our path.
O come; be all in all that we may not be ours but yours
      Because Christ lives in us. Amen.

Peace does not just happen. It occurs by an act of will.
      "Blessed are the PeaceMAKERS," said Jesus.

People Win People

I would be the last to discourage an updating of the membership rolls of our local United Methodist Churches. However, the persistent number of removals would seem to indicate that we are not adequately assimilating, training, and nurturing our members.

Denominationally we are not removing members at a faster rate. We simply are not winning and recruiting new members, in spite of the fact that The United Methodist Church is held in high esteem by our populace.

An observation is that we are not growing because we do not will to do so. Growing requires intentional planning and leadership by our pastors and concerned involvement by laity.

Action plans are underway by our Cabinets. One place to tie into this is for each church to consider an achievable goal of growth and report this in the Charge Conference as a matter of record. Another is for the District Council on Ministries to take this issue seriously through action plans that are to be implemented. We can expect the trend to be reversed if we take seriously the mandate of the Gospel. Remember, someone must make it happen! Let's prepare our people through membership classes and confirmation classes to know that church membership is serious business. Evangelism workshops have not done the job. People win people, and this happens when church membership is exciting and when people decide to tell others.

Each charge and each district has its own situation and its own ideas about how to move out in this enterprise. Help your church become a growing church, in numbers and in Christian experience.

A Word of Thanks to the Cabinets

I want to say a good word about our district superintendents.
These persons who comprise the Cabinets (of both conferences)
with the bishop have been the most conscientious, diligent group
of people you will find in any setting. They don't get the credit they
deserve, and they don't really expect it, but they have worked hard
in hours and in intensity at the appointment process.

We have literally spent days on just one appointment. On all of
them the insights and data provided by Pastor Parish Relations
Committees and congregation members have been evaluated,
weighed, and acted upon. We haven't been happy about all of the
appointments we have made. Churches and pastors are asked to
share with one another the welfare of all of our congregations.

In Cabinet meetings in recent weeks we have witnessed anger,
weariness, and even tears. I have not seen one appointment made
carelessly, lightly, and without awareness of risk and consequence.
Sometimes a charge and a pastor go together like hand and glove.
On other occasions it is a matter of doing the best that can be done
under the circumstances.

Now and then appointments will be put together incorrectly, but
never, I repeat, never, without care and prayerful consideration. I
appreciate our Cabinets. You would, too, if you were to sit in on the
process.

Sometimes we can't do what is best. The best isn't always possible.
But these people care about the pastors and about the churches they
serve.

Without exception, new district superintendents discover a side
of the life of the church they didn't know existed. It is hard work
being a district superintendent. Not all who aspire to that office
know what they would encounter in it. It requires more inner stam-
ina than most imagine.

Some moves are out of necessity. Some are opportunities. Every
time a pastor has to move there are consequences. Another pastor
has to move over. A church has to relinquish its leader. That's our

way. We have responsibilities for one another. Sometimes it works well. Sometimes it doesn't. But the connection, the fellowship of pastors and congregations give and take, cry and rejoice. At the end of the process about 850 churches are provided with the best leadership we can recruit. They begin another year as part of The United Methodist Church. I want to thank our district superintendents for the jillion meetings, encounters, and consultations. They are a group with which I'm glad to be associated.

Annual Conference Is Never the Same

After surgery they call it "post-op." After conferences I suppose we call it "post-conf." It doesn't matter what we call it. I'm in that glad season when the sessions are over, the last amendment has been debated, the delegates have been elected, and the ordination services have been held. It takes one a while to come down from the intensity of trying to maintain the schedule and the orderly rhythm, if there was one. The third day after the adjournment, the weariness of two weeks of "gaveling" begins to emerge. But I write. I mull over the happenings. The bishop asks himself, "How did it go?"

For one thing, a conference doesn't stay the same very long these days. The familiarity one develops suddenly takes on a newness that makes one aware of change. There is an ebb and flow to a conference. Sometimes, over the years, the tide comes in and you feel that a conference is becoming. That is, a personality is taking shape and one thinks one senses what it is.

Then, it is as if the tide moves out, and one sees bits and pieces of refuse that have been abandoned as once having been useful. Attitudes move from one position to another between one delegate election time and another.

Then as the tide moves in again, one knows that the shoreline is not going to be the same. This can be disturbing or challenging, depending on the ability to hope—at least this is my impression.

In many ways we had good conferences. My appreciation for the laity continues to grow. By and large, the laity who come to an Annual Conference are there to help create the church. I believe that once they understand the information, they will exercise appropriate judgment.

There are strange dynamics among preachers. Most are doing the best they can and giving the best leadership they have. They are, in the main, fulfilling their calling.

But an Annual Conference does have a personality. For good or ill, that personality changes in four years. This is partly due to the formation effects of our culture. It is due in some measure to political verities. I must confess that at times I am confused about the quality of our being in covenant as the people of God. In some ways I see more growth in the perception of our laity to the central issues of the church than I do in our pastors. The covenant with God is the measure of all of us.

We have done our deciding, however; and in deciding we have become the Annual Conference we are going to be for at least a few years. Our voting on issues and the processes that went into delegate selection reflect our character as a conference. We have elected good delegations. Unfortunately, there was some hurt. There were dynamics, the effects of which time will reveal. But we are who we are. I don't know of anything more intensive and revealing than Annual Conference in an election year. There were signs of "becoming" and signs of "having been."

The sum of it really rests in the future as we reveal together how able we are to grasp the future and shape it for the sake of Christ. Will we witness? Will we serve? Will we honor Christ? Will we move together or in divided fashion?

Our opportunity is enormous and challenging. The one question we really didn't settle is, "Are we ready to incarnate Christ in ourselves and see Him in each other?"

For each of us, this is our time. We are here. God bless and care for our United Methodist Conferences.

Leave an Old Appointment to the New Minister in All Cases

A matter that has come to my attention merits the direct attention of pastors and the attention of the laity. It has to do with former pastors returning to the former pastorate to perform functions which rightly are the responsibility of the present pastor.

A former pastor should never return to a pastorate to perform weddings, funerals, et cetera, without consulting the present pastor. In fact, the pastor now in charge should never be bypassed by laity in these matters without consulting with the pastor of the church. If it is desired that the former pastor participate in a funeral or wedding, the protocol is that the present minister be asked to invite the former pastor to participate. In the vast majority of cases such a request will be honored.

However, for a previous pastor to succumb to an invitation that would omit consultation with the present pastor is unethical. The pastor who is there now is the pastor of the church. He or she can build the needed relationships to be effective only as that person has the opportunity to provide one's ministry to families, a role that clearly is the role of the appointed pastor.

When a pastor leaves a charge they have served, keys to office, church, and parsonage should be relinquished. There is no other way to do it.

We form loyalties and treasured relationships that are more valuable than gold as we minister to congregations. But, when appointment changes, that congregation becomes the leadership and pastoral turf of the new pastor. A departing pastor should help make this clear to the congregation. This does not discount expressed concern as friend.

It is not intended in this column that treasured friendships are to be cut off. They merely take on a new form. The hospital visitation and the pastoral functions inherent in the pastoral responsibility now belong to the new pastor.

There is a covenant relationship in the ministry which, to be effective, must be honored. It is a covenant strong enough to allow an occasional invitation from the present pastor to a former pastor in certain cases. This can be an amicable relationship or arrangement. For former pastors, however, to claim "ownership" on particular family relationships as if the present pastor did not occupy the "in-charge" responsibility is stretching ministerial ethics too far.

General Conference 1988

Another General Conference is behind us. Or is it? There was an agenda that drove the delegates from morning to night and into the night. Those 996 people elected by the conferences in the United States and from the overseas conferences were a world church at work. It was United Methodism at prayer and at work.

Put in place were the following:

A new hymnal was adopted that is exciting and will help us make a singing church. The statement of doctrine and theology replaces one adopted previously. The stance on homosexuality was retained after nearly four hours of debate. A four-year study of this issue was authorized to help accumulate knowledge and insights on this highly charged issue. After 155 years of history of our church's work on the continent of Africa, the first United Methodist–related university on the continent was overwhelmingly approved. A study of professional ministry was extended for four years. These are only a few of the significant actions taken.

Something else prevailed, however. As one delegate described it, as these two weeks of work and worship preceded, those present became a community of love with their church. The body was determined to make a difference on the future. I was impressed by the spirit of the gathering. It exceeded my expectations. Christ was there.

What we do and what we become is up to us. It wasn't a perfect General Conference, but it will do until a better one comes along. Our Kansas delegations were active participants. Comments from our delegations were of the quality of which I was proud.

We bishops had met for a week in Kansas City ahead of the conference. We had a two-day meeting in St. Louis prior to the con-
vening of the session. The bishops from the autonomous Methodist
Churches (outside the U.S.) met with us. They have so much to
share with us in the states that makes our church better.

The church, ours that is, is growing in long strides in Africa,
China, and Latin America. Theirs is a passion that is contagious.

So here we are, back at home. Compared with so many parts of
the world, we have an abundance with which to work. What a
shame if we do not exhibit greater faithfulness through our discipleship.

Our own vision will be challenged. We will decide again who
we really are in Christ. How big will our issues be? How willing will
we be to risk?

Jurisdictional Conference Results

Jurisdictional Conferences are over. This particular one was of
special significance to me for several reasons. The most personal one
is that Elaine and I were assigned back to Kansas for another four
years. We are glad for this and appreciative of the reception experienced from the delegates and others attending from Kansas.

We had a marvelous though sleepy breakfast together with the
Kansas folk at 6:30 A.M. on Thursday. You wouldn't think a party
could be held at that hour, but it can and it was. So here we are as
we look forward to the next four years in what can be an exciting
time.

At Jurisdictional Conference, the election process of new bishops
and particularly the election itself is indescribable for a bishop-elect.
Upon election one is escorted to the platform. It is a turning point
in one's life. You leave the chair you occupied as a delegate, never to
return to that place and position.

One becomes, upon consecration, a member of the Council of
Bishops. That person is no longer a member of the Annual Conference. The place is changed that one occupies. The position and

responsibility become forever different. Then on the day of consecration, new obligations are recited and vows accordingly are taken.

It is impossible to verbalize the importance of our sending these persons to their new responsibility with our prayers as well as with our love. And, while you are at it, pray for all the bishops. The Lord knows we all need it.

Elaine and I will have the unique experience of being with the fifteen newly elected bishops and their spouses in a week of orientation at Lake Junaluska in a few weeks. I chair the committee in charge of putting the orientation event together.

We will cover such topics as will relate to making the transition, family care in the Episcopal routine, legal guidance, working with Cabinets, the role of the bishop as general superintendent in the church, and other matters that one encounters in this ministry. It won't begin to prepare them for their future labor, but will introduce them to areas of life that will be encountered differently than before.

Jurisdictional Conference was exhausting. It always is. It was exciting. There are things we don't like about this occasion sometimes, but it is the church in motion. Sometimes motion is creative and on occasion it is not. But what is perfect where humans are concerned? GOD BLESS THE UNITED METHODIST CHURCH.

Make a Difference—Give What You Would Like to Receive

It is February, a month when the weather can be bad or fair. Everyone is busy except those who have the flu. The Cabinets are preparing for the regular appointment-making process. There is busyness as well as business going on in the church and in the lives of our people. Everyone has an agenda for themselves and for one another. I am excited as I hear positive things churches are doing. God works with us or in spite of us.

This is the point of this piece. Attitudes are so important and are as catching as the flu that's going around. I have to look at my own attitudes. I have to work on them because there are always people with bad attitudes around who can spoil a day. But now and then an attitude comes along that makes one's day reel with hope and possibilities.

Christians are people who hope. The church's business is to dispense hope. We do that best, it seems to me, when we give hope to someone else we would like to have ourselves. It is a strange thing this giving what you would like to receive.

Most of the problems of our religious life as they pertain to the church are not really the problems of money, organization, or know-how. Much of what detracts from an exciting faith is an absence of trust, faulty relationships, and turning inward. When those factors converge, life becomes negative and our ability to dispense hope is immobilized.

Let us begin to ask what is good about our church: What are we doing well? Who needs our encouragement? And at what point is a positive faith in Jesus Christ needing a hearty witness from us? Is another person being less than that person could be because we are withholding our caring?

A few people who will insist on coming through those questions with a high view of faith can make a difference. I get lots of letters telling me what is wrong with this and that. There are lots of places where the moving creative presence of Christ can transform the climate of life into an affirming center of renewal.

Let's turn it on, United Methodists!! Let's help our pastor to be the best pastor he or she can be. Let's empower our congregation with the good news of Christ. Christians can make the difference if we will decide as Christians, act as Christians, affirm one another as Christians, forgive as Christians, and know that every Christian is a minister. And that means looking outward, looking for opportunity. Someone needs you at our best. The same goes for your church. Let's turn it on!

There Needs to Be a Renewed Emphasis on Preaching

Recently I asked a member of the laity what he sees as some areas of United Methodism that need to be strengthened. Without batting an eye or hesitating for a moment, he replied that there

needs to be a renewed emphasis on preaching. In his opinion, the
Word needs to be proclaimed effectively.

We talked further about this. The more we talked the more I
could see that this was not just an opinion but a conviction. I also
knew that I was agreeing with him.

There is an abundance of help in this area of ministry. An eco-
nomical resource is the series entitled Abington Preacher's Library,
a series of twelve paperback books published in the past two years.
I commend it to our preachers, the whole series.

Just as important, if not more so, is the nurture of a preacher's
center of being. If a preacher doesn't know what this is, my trying
to explain will not help. That hub of life that is what we stand for,
and which identifies us as a communicator of important news, must
have care, prayer, reflection and, ultimately, conviction.

There may be excuses for being only moderately effective as a
preacher, but it is doubtful if there are any for being boring. If the
Gospel of Jesus Christ is not exciting to us as preachers, it can hardly
be to those who sit in the pew.

Another suggestion for preachers is that our assigned place of
ministry, the charge we serve, must be seen as a sacred assignment.
While we are there we have a responsibility for the spiritual nuture
of the flock. That nurture will be defective if we do not claim that
place, that pulpit, and that congregation as a sacred trust.

We should preach as if we are going to be there forever. If we
really want to be somewhere else it will show. If you aren't where
you are, you are nowhere! You aren't with your people and you
aren't in the next place. A hundred people in the worship service is
a hundred hours of that congregation's time.

There is a style that is yours, but the Gospel is God's. It is terribly
important that we tell it as well as we can.

(More on this subject in the chapter entitled "Advice to Pastors.")

The Orientation of the Fifteen

The Orientation of the Fifteen! That's been an exciting experience for Elaine and me. Who were the fifteen? Those were the new

bishops elected by the Jurisdictional Conferences of 1988. These persons with their spouses gathered at Lake Junaluska, the week of September 12, to get acquainted and to share what it is that confronts a new bishop and the family.

The event could not provide all the answers. The episcopacy is not only a position but is also an experience that each must encounter in his or her own life. Our job as a committee, of which I was chair, was to introduce the new leaders to some fundamentals, to provide handles, and to tell them where they might turn for help along the journey.

We engaged in rich worship. We explored family implications. We engaged the roles of the bishop, including that of appointment making, legal implications, working with a Cabinet, and learning what it means to live in professional glass houses and how to manage the precarious fig leaves that both hide and reveal one's strengths and weaknesses.

The group comprised a total of sixty persons, because, you see, we brought on board resource persons from our church at large and bishops who have had long experience upon which to draw. These fifteen persons who have been elected will do well. The church is to be in good hands.

We dealt with "place," which is the daily struggle to ascertain where one is going to place one's self after deciding what one has to omit as well as what is to be included in the overload of expectancy.

We also confronted the reality of "pace" as a bishop determines the balance of adrenalin, stress, and spiritual formation in order to keep a balance as one functions.

Then "presence" was emphasized. For me, this is the realization with the Psalmist that God sometimes seems to be silent, yet is never absent. To confuse the two is to lose the glow.

For all of us, to keep faith in the midst of waves of change and adversity is to know that while we may languish for some word from God, God is never absent from the scene where life is engaged.

That fresh realization in the midst of this splendid group was my gift of grace. I hope it is yours.

Pray for the fifteen and for all of us who continue.

Preparing for Retirement

So much is happening so fast in the lives of Elaine and me these days. Attending the Council of Bishops meeting and General Conference involved three weeks; Annual Conferences occupied two weeks. Bishop's Week at Mount Sequoyah included not only the program, but also an interview with the Jurisdictional Episcopacy Committee, plus a full day of meeting with the Jurisdictional College of Bishops.

It's tempting to say, "Hold on! I'm getting ready to retire—or trying to get ready." We do not have to be out of here by August 31. The new bishop will commence his or her assignment beginning on September 1.

We want to thank the folks of Kansas for the tremendous celebrations of retirement which were so well planned and so interesting. Thank you for the gifts from the conferences and the personal messages. We will remember our associations with great fondness. My Kansas roots have taken on new meaning during these eight years with you as bishop.

We all know that there was much that didn't get done. I am probably aware of that more surely than most. One is spread too thin. But another bishop will bring a new perspective, new interests, and a new style. It will be good.

The agenda of the summer has been heavier than expected. We still have appointments to make, personnel matters to clear. Each day brings a surprise.

In the meantime, in this move, Elaine and I are trying to weed out after forty-six years of marriage and ever so many other moves in which we transported things around. So this time of moving is a mixed one. We are casting away, keeping what is dear, cutting the "maybe we'll need it someday" stuff. It is emotional as well as physical.

We will move practically all of our goods the week of July 20. That will give the Residence Committee time to do some work on the house. The new bishop will visit Topeka sometime the latter part of July to survey the living details. I will spend some personal orientation time with that person. So will Sharon Wagoner. Elaine and I will be around during August. The tasks will take me down to the wire it appears.

After September 1 our address will be:

3909 South Lookout

Little Rock AR 72205

Phone: 501-663-9670

This may not be my last piece in the paper, but at least you have this word of deep gratitude and our plans about the days just ahead.

Editor's note: The following excerpts were taken from an article written by the Topeka Capital-Journal reporter Mark Enoch upon the imminent retirement of Bishop Hicks from the Episcopacy of The United Methodist Church effective September 1, 1992.

Bishop to Stay Active in Church

Even though Methodist Bishop Kenneth W. Hicks will retire Sept. 1 after 43 years as an active minister, he seems destined to remain an influence in the United Methodist Church.

Hicks, 69, and his wife, Elaine, plan to move to Little Rock, AR, where he will have an office in a 4,000-member church as a volunteer "bishop-in-residence." He plans to teach and possibly work with Heifer Project International, a program which seeks to bring improved agriculture skills to other countries.

As the bishop for Kansas, Hicks presided over about 760 Methodist churches from his office in Topeka. It is a lifetime away from his childhood on a farm near Iola.

Hicks grew up in the United Brethren Church, which later became part of The United Methodist Church. He graduated from high school in 1941, just six months before America entered World War II.

He first served a Methodist church while a student in 1946. He was graduated from a Denver seminary in 1953 and his first church after graduation, in Pueblo, CO, had a multi-racial congregation of blacks, whites and Japanese.

Hicks became a bishop in Arkansas in 1976, and moved to Topeka in 1984.

Hicks has seen the church and the world undergo immense changes since his high school days.

He has watched the erosion of trust in institutions, including churches.

"I think it's hard to be a leader for any institution today, including the church," Hicks said. "The church has let itself be shaped by the culture of our society."

Instead, Hicks believes the gospel is meant to be a change agent for society by dealing with current problems. "The intent of the gospel of Jesus Christ is to empower us to change God's world," Hicks said.

The United Methodist Church, like most mainline Protestant denominations, has lost members during the past generation. That especially threatens the existence of smaller churches.

In Kansas, about two-thirds of the Methodist churches have fewer than 200 members. Hicks said that some churches will close, while others will find a new vitality if they have a vision for their purpose.

"We're not delivering religion in the same way than in the 1950s—that won't work," he said. "The church has got to become more contemporary in our agenda."

Hicks said more congregations may need to share ministers or use the services of part-time ministers. He also expects to see more lay leadership.

Hicks would like to see churches focus more on spreading the Gospel, instead of focusing on health in numbers or dollars. "The Christian Gospel was never intended to be an institution," Hicks said. "The Christian Gospel was intended to be a movement."

CHAPTER
9

Easter

Palm Sunday Congregation

Celebration is the theme.
Where are the celebrants in this congregation?
Tired faces bearing tired ruts of
    Same smiles, same frown, same cares.
The lines in the faces are not the lines of direction,
    But ruts of sameness.
They are not lines of design, but wrinkles
    Of dormancy.
Break open the morning, you who worship!
Break it open as a new box of candy.
Eat of it, consume it.
Burn up the energy it provides.

The sermon I'm hearing tells of God's caring,
    God's kingdom, of denial.
Hosanna means "hello," "welcome."

My life, I must decide, will be open to new lines.
My wrinkles will not be ruts, but scars,
For the celebration of Palm Sunday is
    The festival of risk.

God, help me to know when to cleanse the temple of my life
    With indignation, and when to surrender my life to
    The healing of your love.
            KWH

Jesus Made a Difference

As we move through the Lenten season, the reading of scripture and other materials related to this special time seem to stand out in vivid fashion in a special way. That is what this piece is about.

A reading of the Gospels, for instance, clearly reveals that what Jesus was about was serious business. The short ministry of Jesus was demonstrated in a way that declared His intention to make a difference.

If Jesus had been interested in small stuff, He would not have been killed. It was not so much a platform or program that consumed Him as it was to declare the reign of God in human affairs. I think if Jesus were a minister today, He would focus on the will of God for this time. His religion would be proclaimed so as to speak to the meaning of life, its purpose, and what He believes to be appropriate responses to the human predicament.

Jesus was not a "maintenance" person. He cared for the deprived and the depraved. Every occasion of His coming into contact with persons was to make known the spirit of God.

Jesus gave evangelism and evangelicalism a unique twist. The only motive He provided for people coming to Him was to be liberated for obedience. Where institutions—religious and secular—were in the way of compassion, He chose compassion. He broke the law, but he broke it upward to a new level of experience in God.

Jesus made it tough for the church and for the government. People were always having to choose their points of loyalty. Jesus made a difference.

It is my prayer that the gift of this season will be so real as to enable and empower our choices upward in faith, trust, and compassion.

I don't often recommend movies, at least in print, but one you should see is *Cry Freedom*. In the struggle in South Africa, as told in this story, you will see a lesson that can be applied to most of the world. It is, "we can make a difference."

Sometimes it is costly, but that is the story of the cross. But I believe the cross is what Christianity is meant to be. It is picking up that which is out of order, sinful, tedious, and unfair, and by our life seek to make a difference.

Following Jesus Is Difficult

Easter will soon be here. The Lenten season is a time of drama for the spirit if we can hold our spiritual hearts above the drowning waters of church meetings long enough to worship.

Lent is the season of stark remembrance of approximately six weeks of raw confrontation on the part of Jesus, who, through a lifestyle of love and justice, challenged with His life the established idols of Caesar and organized religion. Jesus and the disciples were on a march of soul of which only Jesus knew the route.

He would show up at a well, a refreshment-deficient party, in church or in an encounter with a handicapped person, leaving them in a state of surprise.

Jesus wasn't predictable. He spoke of life as if it is sacred. He applied the proprieties of religion as if there is no love without justice. Politics was forced to face up to its effects. Decency and human worth had priority in His life.

Respect for Caesar was not automatic if Caesar was not moral. Religious precept was not compromised by a demand for patriotism above righteousness.

It is still difficult to be firm on behalf of the people if policies have to be critiqued as to their impact on human beings. I have experienced that. It is refreshing to hear words from the president which indicate an awareness of the environment, the homeless, the need for greater sensitivity for the cause of children, and word in favor of self-determination by peoples of the world. Maybe the dawn of Easter will bring an influx of hope. Easter can do it if we let it.

Gustavo Gutierrez closes his book, *We Drink from Our Own Wells,* with the following: "Spirituality is a community enterprise. It is the passage of a people through the solitude and dangers of the desert, as it carves out its way in the following of Jesus Christ. This spiritual experience is the well from which we must drink. From it we draw the promise of resurrection."

It's Called Compassion

> *And Jesus went about all the cities and villages, teaching in their synagogues and preaching the gospel of the kingdom, and healing every disease and every infirmity. When he saw the crowds, he had compassion for them, because they were harassed and helpless, like sheep without a shepherd. Then he said to his disciples, "The harvest is plentiful, but the laborers are few; pray therefore the Lord of the harvest to send out laborers into his harvest."*
> *—Matthew 9:35–38*

In a day when bucks and votes seem to be uppermost in matters shaping public policy, who speaks on behalf of people? In both Old and New Testament, there is weighty evidence that the nature and personality of God always endeavor to speak up for people. In the leadership of the prophets and later, in the clear light of Jesus' life, the lesson is vivid and full of impact: in Jesus we see that God wants to uphold the interests of human beings.

In the verses above we see that Jesus was in solidarity with people, and being in such a stance, He was moved to compassion.

A book that has moved me greatly for several years is titled *The Prophetic Imagination*. The author, Walter Brueggeman, says that "compassion constitutes a radical form of criticism, for it announces that the hurt is to be taken seriously, that hurt is not to be accepted as normal and natural, but is an abnormal and unacceptable condition for humanness."

There are so many examples of Jesus speaking for people through His compassion. The scripture above notes that "when he saw the crowds, he had compassion for them because they were harassed and helpless." Or in Luke 7 where we are told of a grieving mother whose son has died: "And when the Lord saw her, he had compassion on her."

We must not forget the Good Samaritan who wasn't even supposed to be doing church work anyway; yet, he was the one held up for notice because of what he did while some church people passed by.

A look in your concordance under "compassion" will so overwhelm you with compassion as a characteristic of a Christ follower that we can't escape the assignment. There is someone or some people who need us to speak on their behalf; to speak for people as Christ speaks for people. Compassion is both the pain and the glory of Lent.

Writing this during Holy Week, a nudge of the Spirit comes through to remind me that whatever is lacking in Christian impact (and much is lacking indeed), there is the assurance of *Resurrection* at the heart of what we do. The impact of our witness may be faulty, but the reality beyond the cross is too much to be silent about.

Let us be reminded that the Spirit uses deliberate intentions and plans which are designed with care. God also uses that which hasn't occurred to us yet. To be fully human is to be aware of God and the possibilities for growing as Christians.

Easter and the Stone before the Tomb

Easter is supposed to be a day of excitement for Christians, and it has been for me. There are some troubling thoughts that flow across the ripples of my mind on this day, nevertheless.

What I'm thinking about is the modeling of meanness and hatred that seems to be so prevalent. And we wonder why there is the rising rate of crime, violence, and gangs. There is a lot of mean-spirited action being foisted upon our society in the name of righteousness.

We must respect those who oppose our positions, but we must go further and respect one another. Intimidation, ridicule, and threats are not the way of righteous people.

What is happening is that hatred is on the rise. Elie Wiesel, holocaust victim and Nobel Peace Prize winner in 1986, says that "an idea becomes fanatical the moment it minimizes or excludes all the ideas that confront or oppose it ...The fanatic never rests and never quits; the more he conquers, the more he seeks new conquests. For him to feel free, he must put everyone else into prison—if not physically, at least mentally."

Wiesel says that our only way to disarm hatred is by celebrating, cherishing, and defending the liberty of others—of all others. So much is at stake. Religious fanaticism is the worst kind it seems to me. Even negative descriptions of pastors by congregations sometimes would curl your hair. It may be because one is a woman, a member of another race, or because one is single.

If we can't always have our way, can't we reflect the resurrection spirit? The moment I hate I have become like them. The moment I love I rise a step toward God. The height, little as it is, makes those who hate seem small.

When the resurrection occurred, Jesus the Christ became something we never fully understood. But though He is with us, He is also something for me to rise toward. He seems to make things new and gives us a new view of humanity. If God could take that kind of chance on us and respect us frail creatures, maybe our job is to keep rolling that stone away. Don't let it stay in front of the tomb.

Songs to Dispel the Darkness

As we begin our fifth summer in Arkansas, a note of sadness hangs in the air around our place on South Lookout. The past four years we have experienced the coming of a Chuck-Will's Widow down in the woods. On April 15 around 10:00 P.M. he (or she) has started a cheerful nighttime call that was bright and boisterous. We looked forward to it every night during the month or so the bird was around. The darkness of the woods back of our house would take on the gladness.

I wonder if the hot summer got him or if he got old and died. We wish we would hear that call again. It made night time a pleasure. Sometimes he would start his serenade later and even awaken us. We didn't mind. He would break the night time and somewhat orchestrate the darkness with a bright note of hope for tomorrow.

Familiar friends and colleagues have the opportunity to do that all the time for one another. We all need it. Why not do it? Songs in the night are a matter of record. Jesus and the disciples sang a hymn before the darkness of Gethsemane. Paul and Silas sang songs in the night.

Sometimes when staff members are gone I realize that around the Council offices some things reassuring and supportive are missing. As the Annual Conference approaches we will gather to be who we are and decide what we are.

Congregations count on us. We count on one another. Issues literally reach out to us for some insight and implementation. Hunger, evangelism, the death penalty, education—all are issues at the heart of which are human beings.

There is an air of darkness surrounding the hopes of many people. It manifests itself in cynicism, distrust, and a longing for a caring word.

It's past midnight as this is written. I've been doing paperwork, doing dictation, getting ready to be out of the state for the Council of Bishops meeting in South Dakota and meetings of boards of trustees at St. Paul Seminary and Southern Methodist University before I return.

All of a sudden I miss that old bird out there in the woods. But you know what? It's Easter morning and shortly millions of people will be assembling to celebrate another song, "Hallelujah, Christ is risen!" Ah, there it is, not a bird, but a Presence. The darkness is about to surrender its hold. We are not alone.

Possibilities After Easter?

What is possible after Easter? What difference does it make? Let me suggest one difference it makes for me.

Two things I feel as burdens—uncertainty and change. Their size and awesome presence overwhelm me. They are the giants with which I deal. They comprise the leviathan of today. They seize all my attention and strain every ounce of who I am, and strangely, I am glad.

To have to strain the sinews of spirit and intellect; to put shoulder to the boulders that would roll over me; to move the boulders when necessary in order to make room for a new world. Ah! That is life in challenging form.

Because of Easter, I will pit my faith and God's ability to work through me against the uncertain and changing movements and overwhelm them with the mighty love and presence of a living creative God. This is the difference Easter makes. May its gift be our togetherness as the church.

Easter will continue with God making crosses only a costly reminder of the servanthood required to empty tombs of doom and replace them with life of abundant grace. The world will still be imperfect. We will still have to decide about the hungry, whether or not there is peace, and whether or not justice prevails. We will still have to decide whether it is enough to believe or if the Gospel is a mandate for action.

The hint I get from Easter is that it is the latter.

CHAPTER
10

"He's Got the Whole World in His Hands"

Let's Make a Difference

I believe we can do better as United Methodists
    than we are doing.
God is calling us to the future.
We must assure one another as we name our fears
And describe what God is calling us to do.

As United Methodists we have much in place,
But we must break the chains of impoverishment
And claim space for Christ.
We must look at the servanthood implied
    in a Christlike ministry,
        And at the covenant we share.
              KWH

Editor's note: The following was presented by Bishop Hicks at
a United Methodist Conference in Dallas, Texas, on March 4,
1983, concerning ethnic inclusiveness as a denominational
priority within The United Methodist Church. The purpose of
the priority was to enhance the impact and witness of ethnic
minority congregations. As forward thinking as it was at the
time it was presented, the church would do well to reread it
periodically.

Developing and Strengthening the Ethnic Minority Local Church

Developing and strengthening the ethnic minority local church,
whatever else the priority has done for The United Methodist
Church, it has joined our church to the twentieth century. It has
been the vehicle by which we have gained a fresh reminder that
God is sovereign ruler of all existence and being; that Jesus Christ
is the unique expression of God's love, care, and concern for the
destiny of humanity; that the Holy Spirit is God's continuous presence with human beings, wooing them and enabling them to
respond with faith, hope, love, and compassion; that the church, the
body of Christ, is the community of faith through which Christians
witness and serve, and constantly lift before the world God's plan of
salvation; that human beings of all ethnic, cultural, racial, and social
backgrounds are of equal value and worth; and that all human beings
are guilty of sin and are in constant need of being challenged "to do
what is just, to show constant love, and to live in humble fellowship
with our God" (Micah 6:8).

Much of the previous statement is from the preface of the hand-
book prepared to set forth the substance of the priority.

You know as well as I the nature of the accomplishments of the
priority. New churches have been built, old churches have been
improved, leadership has been enabled. Not all has been accomplished which should have been; but time is not yet at an end. There
is a vocabulary in our church language now that declares an awareness of others in a way not previously used. There is the known factor that God's people are brown, tan, black, red, and white. The

world is mostly un-Christian yet, but Christ is alive. We have seen Him in faces and congregations and enterprises that have added to the identity of each of us and of all of us together.

I believe it has been the intention of God that we have this priority. We have left undone much that should have been done. We have done some things that should not have been done. But to the extent that we have been faithful, we have been enriched as people and as the body of Christ. Therefore, there is much to celebrate. There is cause for rejoicing and there is ample agenda for the future.

I have before me two objects. One is a watch, which symbolizes that there is a flow of time in which we stand. If we are spiritual people, we know that it is God's time. We have been in it. We are in it. It is our time in which to repent, to celebrate, and to plan for the future. The other object is a compass. We have found ourselves experiencing not only a priority but also a direction. A direction has no end. It is only an indicator of stance. It points the way of a journey that is not yet completed. The important thing is not whether we have reached the intended goal, but are we facing the right direction?

It seems to me to be imperative that we know both the time and direction, for the quest that has engaged us is not a four-year journey, but a lifetime of response. God is still creating. We are needed in that creative event.

Of all that has been done, and there is much, Manuel Expareto is right when he said, "The greatest strength of The United Methodist Church is to be attained when we at once affirm our separate heritages and identify and commit to these with ourselves in celebration of our union in Christ . . ." (e/sa May 1981, 15). So is Thom Fassett correct when he writes: "The United Methodist Church is beginning to clarify a vision which speaks of the Gospel of Jesus Christ bringing wholeness and knitting together the social fabric of human existence . . . The United Methodist Church is beginning to understand that such a mission will bring wholeness to the church and, therefore, not only strengthen the ethnic minority church but others as well" (e/sa May 1981, 13).

So I suggest that we affirm the journey, be sure of our direction, know that our time is God's time, and prepare for a journey of excitement and momentum. Let us seize the direction toward which God has set us. Let us encompass this moment of time that is our life, give it God's shape and cast it upon the future as people who know whose they are and what they must do. Let us celebrate the distance we have come for we have come this far by faith.

So much for the celebration.

Now, for the future. And the time to begin that future is now. The tenor of our time is one with sharp edges. A hard line approach is too much the style by which our political leadership approaches most problems. Unfortunately, problems involve people. The human equation cannot be met just by budgets, recessions, armaments, and defense spending. Those are functional terms, when relational terms of love, peace, justice, caring, and supporting are the real deficits of our age.

The world is comprised of problem solvers and planners. I believe the Bible is a book for planners, for those who have a vision, who have been caught up in the intention of God and are restless to know what it is.

Without regard to our deciding, there are responses of reaction or intervention. Reaction is confrontation, dissatisfaction, crabbing, heel nipping, and belly-aching in general. Intervention is having a dream and looking for the potential to fill it; having a vision and a sense of commitment to know the risk of changing that which ought to be changed.

I have a frivolous whim that consists of the enjoyment of the western novels of Louis L'Amour. These tales of the old west are light reading. I usually take one along to read on the plane on the way home from meetings when more serious reading is out of the question. They are stories of good guys and bad guys. There is shooting and fighting. I like them. You see, I'm probably not as nonviolent as I like to think I am any more than I am probably not as nonracist as I like to think I am. So, there you are. The bishop has divested himself of his ecclesiastical garments and stands before you exposed.

I don't always like just holy books, and like to share the imaginary adventures of "shoot 'em up, take them over, and bring order to the territory." So now you know. You have glimpsed my vulnerability, something a bishop is never supposed to allow.

This is probably where we are as a church. Anyhow, to return to the profundity of this presentation. One of L'Amour's books entitled *The Ferguson File* has a scene in which one of the characters says, "Here and there I heard talk of Oregon and California. Once a man has made that first move, once he has cast off his moorings, his associations, his churches, his village store, and his relatives, it is easy to continue on. It is always easier to travel than to stop. As long as one travels toward the promised land, the dream is there, to stop means to face the reality; and it is easier to dream than to realize the dream."

I think there is a word here about the ethnic minority local church. We have had a dream. Jesus had a dream. There are instances in which Jesus said we have to cast off the moorings, put our hands to the plow and not look back, drink the cup that He drinks, enlarge the family of mother and brothers to include others.

Jesus had the ability to stop and bind the wounded, release the captive, love the unloving. It is at the moment when the dream must be held, not to escape the reality, but to deal with it. It was those moments, those occasions when while possessing the dream, He stopped because of the dream, to do what was demanded, that held the risk that ultimately led to his demise.

Jesus knew what time it was and He had his direction clear. His style was a style of inclusiveness that didn't ask people to become what they couldn't, but to help them become what they could. This was a style not of reaction but of intervention. Intervention challenges the systems, the ways we have done things. Intervention spreads the responsibility of who is in charge.

Tax collectors, fishermen, prostitutes, shepherds, Samaritans, even people from afar visited the manger of Christ's birth. There is not the slightest doubt that all people of God's creation were and are God's children.

When Jesus was born, modern media standards would assume that the announcement would be made in public ornate surroundings. Actually the announcement was made to the shepherds. They were the ones who heard the angels' song. These non-status people received the news and made their way to the most unlikely place, a stable. There, tucked away in straw was one who when they saw Him, they believed they were seeing something of God.

Christ, we have learned in this priority, resides in the unexpected, the unlikely, the marginalized places and people of society. Thus, when Christ is experienced in the Asian, the American Indian, the African, the Hispanic, and Caucasian, there is a uniqueness of revelation that enriches all.

When rightly understood, the impact of the Christian message is not so much in what Christ says about the poor. He is the poor. Not so much in what he says about the oppressed. He is the oppressed. Not so much in what he says about humanity. He is humanity. Not so much in what he says about peace. He is even the Prince of Peace.

There is part of my salvation that is not complete until He is known by all. Part of my redemption awaits the redemption of all.

Before this Missional Priority there was a tendency to believe we understood the fullness of God. He was ours, and by ours was meant *ours, mine; not yours, not your kind.* This priority has awakened us to the knowledge that there is a part of God that I will never have or know until he or she is included in the package of totality.

I cannot know God as I need to know God until American Indians extend that gift in their unique package, their unique culture. I wander in lostness until God is expressed through personalities of every background. What is most pertinent in this occasion is that The United Methodist Church can never be the church it is meant to be until its Lord is expressed in every ethnic culture. Maybe this hints as to how we will find our identity as a church.

Let me tell you of an experience my wife and I had this past fall. There is an elderly man who lives with a family across the street from us. He has been with them for years. He is impaired in speech. He limps. He is old. Either through age or disadvantage his functions and activities are very elementary. One morning he was doing as he usually did during the fall season. Each morning at daybreak he would be outside with his broom sweeping up the leaves along the curb in front of the house where he lives. In fact, he usually swept most of the street. On this particular morning shortly after daybreak, I looked out and there he was, sweeping the leaves in the curb with an old broom long since worn out. There were so few straws left on it that he was using the broom horizontally rather than vertically to move the leaves. As he approached our side of the street with his disheveled broom, my wife told me to take him one of our brooms. We both felt the travesty of his kindness with the old tool he was using. I went out with my broom and said, "Roosevelt, this is so kind of you. At least take this broom. And thank you so much for what you are doing."

His response was one of profuse gratitude that I would give him a better broom to sweep up my leaves, an act that was purely of his own volition. We thanked each other, but his gratitude was so profuse and so pure that I was moved. He considered that I was doing him a favor in making what he wanted to do easier to do.

This weighed on me all day until it broke in upon me what I had experienced. I ultimately knew that in that earnest face and jumbled speech I had seen the face and spirit of Jesus. I truly believe that in that act of servanthood I saw Jesus.

This is symbolic of what I believe the Gospel to mean. Without his knowing it, he incarnated that which added to my experience of Christ. He placed the vision of inclusiveness in a moment of confrontation, and I was enabled to look at my theology and myself, and I was blessed. Those formally considered marginalized people are God's people. I cannot say that I am saved until I share their salvation in their faces, in their deeds, in their cultures.

It does not appear that the present priority in its present form will be the design of the priority of the next quadrennium. But I say to you, there can be no real evangelism without including all people and no congregational development without designing formats appropriate to all our cultures and racial backgrounds.

I do not know what God intends to do with The United Methodist Church. I don't know if we are going to increase in numbers or not. Maybe if we maintain our dream while we stop to minister to reality, we will result in a church half the size we now have. But I do know that we cannot and dare not simply try to reclaim the statistics of 1968 with white designs.

I will go a step further and say that there can be no authentic evangelism without justice. Justice is as integral a part of evangelism as it is of politics.

In 1980 we approved a financially anemic special program called "Peace with Justice"; but at least we recognized that there can be no lasting peace, no shalom peace, without justice. I think we could do worse than to brazenly say we are at a juncture where it is appropriate to use the phrase "Evangelism and Church Growth with Justice."

This will radically alter the nature of evangelism; but are we going to intervene or react? Jesus did not advocate a melting pot. He acknowledged and welcomed diversity. And He became the center whereby diversity could find unity. It was the denial of this principle by the established church of his day that caused his crucifixion.

Let me parenthetically illustrate this more radical dimension by the issue of open itineracy. Open itineracy is an established policy in our church. *It is not an established practice.*

I know of few areas where bold examination and challenge must become the agenda of bishops and superintendents than this. It works both ways. It means opening historically ethnic pulpits to whites and others. It means opening historically white pulpits to blacks and others. God assumes us to be one people—God's people. Radical changes.

So I humbly but pointedly say that inclusiveness requires a more radical approach to theology than we have experienced to date. A radical church is one that learns how to do the necessary. It is one that is willing to learn and see. It is one that knows it is not enough

any longer to believe. *We must obey.* It is not enough to worship—
we must follow. It is not enough to be personally saved—we must
be aware of the corporate responsibility of being the people of God.
It is no longer enough to know what the Bible says. *We must ask
of each other, "What does it mean?"*

A radical church knows that our real God is not just the one we
worship, but also the one who shapes and influences decisions. (Acts
12: "Peter continued knocking.")

We have seen the vision. We have caught a glimpse these past few
years as to what we can become. God, give us courage not only to
have the dream, but also to stop by the scenes of reality containing
a world of multifaceted cultures. Let us build our churches, share our
faith, and keep knocking.

CHAPTER
11

Advice to Pastors . . .

Healing Waters

Let these waters heal me, Lord.
The noise of life has almost overcome me.
Let the noise of the waves crowd out the wounds
        caused by the dashing waves of the world.
These waves heal.
They exist because beneath,
        in the support of the lake bed,
        open palms are there holding in place
        the grandeur I have seen today.

Three o'clock waves seem to be so cleansing, at least today.
They wash away the cares we write on the sands as if to say,
        "Life doesn't hold these against you."
Begin again.
Go away from here forgiven.
You are accepted, though imperfect.
Which one is the perfect wave?
Which is the perfect breeze?
Which ray of sun is the one without blemish of dust or cloud?
So my life is not without blemish either;
But it is my life.
If I offer it to the good of all life,
        "That is sufficient."
Thus said the Lord to me today.

KWH

Put Style in Your Ministry

There is a little paperback book I found years ago which was
never mentioned in seminary while I was there, but it contains gems
of insight, which I wish I had been ordered to deal with. It's called
Letters to a Young Poet by Rainier Maria Rilke. Rilke was a Euro-
pean writer who died in 1926. This small volume is his letters, written over thirty years before, to an aspiring young poet. I want to
paraphrase a bit of what he wrote to the young poet using the language of preaching instead of the language of writing.

"You ask whether your sermons are good . . . You compare them
to other sermons, and you are disturbed when certain hearers reject
your efforts. Now . . . I beg you to give up all that. You are looking
outward, and that above all you should not do now . . . Go into
yourself. Search for the reason that bids you preach: find out
whether it is spreading out its roots in the deepest places of your
heart, acknowledge to yourself whether you would have to die if it
were denied you to preach. This above all—ask yourself in the stillest
hour of your night: must I preach? Delve into yourself for a deep
answer. And if this should be affirmative, if you may meet this earnest
question with a strong and simple, "I must," then build your life
according to this necessity; your life even into its most indifferent
and slightest hour must be a sign of this urge and a testimony to it."

With reference to writing, Rilke is talking about the necessity of
the writer finding the degree to which that old-fashioned word
"unction" is present, and if it is, then developing a life that gives an
authentic sign to this urge so as to become a testimony to it. I take
that to mean "style." I'm not talking about buttons and hair, gestures
or no gestures, sweating or not sweating when you preach.

Something more basic is at stake which must come from those
deep caverns of who we are until, as Rilke says, "your life even into
its most indifferent and slightest hour must be a sign of this urge and
a testimony to it."

Contemporary life is fraught with that which persuades us to live
in the shallows rather than in the depths. I came into the living
room recently while a commercial was being recited on television.

I wanted to say something important to Elaine, so I didn't even look at the television screen. As I started to speak, I realized I was competing with someone who seemed to be saying to my nonattentiveness, "This leg has been shaved with Brand X, this leg has been shave with Brand Proper. Therefore, look your delectable best in your bikini this summer. Keep your legs looking great with Brand Proper." For a split second, I thought, "do you suppose it's possible?" Then I gained my senses and went ahead with the conversation. The one giving the commercial message had been talking with such vigor and excitement you would have thought a bulletin had just given the time and place of the rapture.

That's not the quality of style I'm talking about, not even that style held by an artist or singer. I'm concerned about style as it begins to capture the meaning of life, one's coordination of abilities, and the projection of values.

The style of the pastor is in some degree a skill like some of those I have mentioned. We know that pastoring and preaching are expressed in differing ways. Basically though, style as I am using it is a total way of living. It has to do with the ways by which and the values by which we authentically manifest our total way of living as ministry.

Servanthood with Justice

> Behold my servant, whom I uphold, my chosen, in whom
> my soul delights; I have put my Spirit upon him, he will
> bring forth justice to the nations. He will not cry or lift up
> his voice, or make it heard in the street; a bruised reed he
> will not break, and a dimly burning wick he will not
> quench; he will faithfully bring forth justice. He will not
> fail or be discouraged till he has established justice in the
> earth; and the coastlands wait for his law.
> —Isaiah 42:1–4

There are several givens in the above passage that reflect God's

style, characteristics of God's mission. The job description described
by God indicates that the minister will be a servant. The word is
used presumably because there is none other that correctly describes
the life to be lived. Servanthood—not prima donna, not a star, not
somebody who lives off the security of the appointive system—but
servanthood.

Then God says, "I have put my spirit on him." Which is to say,
that the motivation for servanthood will by its nature and the nature
of the one who is servant spread itself into the very roots of the
heart—a heart permeated by a spirit that is God's. We are not on our
own. We are not *even* our own. We are bearers of a spirit given as a
gift of grace.

Walking around this passage and looking at it from another side,
this description of God's style says that the servanthood needed is
one which will have as its single aim that of bringing justice to the
nations—an interesting description of ministry, a strange word for
which we usually use the word "salvation." We may like "salvation"
better because it is less demanding and carries less risk.

You have to remember that in the world of Isaiah there was
oppression. For oppressed people, justice is the appropriate word for
salvation, as is bread for a hungry world. Isaiah believes God is saying
that in a world containing oppressed people ministry must be called
"justice." You can get saved and re-saved, but until that salvation
manifests itself in an urgency for justice, our ministry is narrow. It is
like a rusty bucket that can hold no water.

Servanthood with Certitude

Walking on around this text, the Lord says, "the coastline waits for
his law." There is a waiting public out there. Ministry in a day that
contains isolation, desolation, oppression and depression, exile and
elitism—well, God says, "For this I need a servant."

Now, looking away from the description that tells us where God
stands, let's look at this servant that is called in a day of spiritual dry
bones. What is he or she to be like? Supposing we say, "Well, surely,
ministry will have a Master's of Divinity; at least, he or she will out-

shine, out-statistic, out-innovate the average." No, that's not the language.

Remember, the Lord is looking for someone who has the capacity to instill hope, to lead a nation into restoration, and who actually makes a piece of the world a little better.

And how will the servant do it? He really doesn't say. Servant implies caring and serving, but how that's done he leaves unspecified.

He just talks about style. The servant will not cry or lift up his voice. Out-shouting one another seems inappropriate. "A bruised reed he will not break." That carries an awareness of the sacredness of life. And he or she won't be windy enough to quench a dimly burning wick. He won't fail or be discouraged.

These are negative comments that stand out with positive affirmation as to style. This is not to suggest that the servanthood is to be dull or passive. It appears, too, that its vitality is to be found in a style of certitude.

Servanthood in Pastoral Style

Henri Nouwen says, "Jesus was a revolutionary who did not become an extremist, since he did not offer an ideology, but Himself. He was also a mystic who did not use his intimate relationship with God to avoid the social evils of his time, but shocked his milieu to the point of being executed as a rebel." That, my friends, is style!

The task is uncompromising. The style by which the task is demonstrated must be no less filled with self-confidence about ourselves and about God. But, abounding is the face that the spirit of the Lord has been shared as a gift of grace. And the mandate is to set humanity free from sin in all its forms. Therefore, we do not set our rhythm by the pronouncements of halls of legislature or pressure groups, but by the claim of Almighty God.

Style abhors frothy, shallow treatment of scripture; style must not back down from the Master's description of his own call: "The Spirit of the Lord is upon me, because he has anointed me to preach good news to the poor. He has sent me to proclaim release to the captives and recovering of sight to the blind, to set at liberty those who are oppressed, to proclaim the acceptable year of the Lord." Which is to say, that now is the time when servanthood must examine everything we are hiding behind in our society and the idols in which we proclaim our faith.

And in what style? In the style of a servanthood pastor whose sense of nonviolence is not enough to break a damaged reed. It is gentle enough not to blow out a flickering wick. But it is tough enough to know that the accountability of such servanthood is to God.

Ordained through Community

Let's walk around Isaiah 42:1–4 in the opposite direction. In United Methodist terminology, we have tradition; we have scripture; we have reason; we have experience. We believe these are extensions by which style can be manifested. It becomes important for ministry precisely as we absorb them in such a way, embody them in such a way, that we use them for the skill of ministry. We bring a great variety of experiences to bear in such a way that they form a whole—they go together to create a way of being, a way of living. That's what I mean by style.

In your case, as a United Methodist minister, we are now talking about a particular tradition, a particular scripture, a particular set of experiences—yours and Methodism's. These, with your reason, have gone together to create a life story which is yours. It is to be expressed in our life and ministry style.

A lot has gone into this. I hope you appreciate the corporate life of which you are a part. You are here because you have had your integrity affirmed by the community of faith. You have experienced the affirmation of a local church, a district committee, a board of ordained ministry and your Annual Conference. *Your call has been endorsed by the community.*

That tradition has been no little factor in bringing you here, and the community called United Methodism has a right to expect your integrity in living out that endorsement.

To be a United Methodist minister means something in particular, and that tradition has a right to hold you accountable for a considerable measure of loyalty to it. You have a right to change it for the better. You do not have a right to undermine it. Every denomination has its identity and personality. Ours does also. To transgress the sacredness of the personality of the community that nurtured you is as much a sin as to transgress the personality of an individual to whom you are a pastor.

Administering the Sacraments

Moving a bit further around the text, we realize the reality of its sacraments. Your style manifests itself in a pronounced way in the manner in which you conduct the sacraments. In those sacraments, you assist in intrusion of the Real Presence into the present so that the present manifests evidence of the *real presence of God.* Teach their meaning. They are part of the gift of God's spirit spoken of in the text. Don't tack them on. Don't dilute or relegate them flippantly as a necessary, but interruptive, time-taker from more "important" things. They, too, are the tradition. They come from scripture.

Let your reason and your experience give you a style that says, when you baptize a person or offer communion: "This matters!" The sacraments are no place to show your speed. When you do, it appears that your mind wants to get somewhere else. Your style of servanthood will be manifested in your understanding and ministration of the sacraments as few other places show it. How careless or careful you are with the sacraments reveal the measure of your ministry's validity.

Preaching as Theological Encounter

Walk a step further around the text. If you don't break reeds and blow out faint wicks of faith, how do you preach? Well, you don't just preach. Anyone with a gift of gab can preach. Your style must preach the Word of God. The communities of our conferences are hungry to remember the mighty acts of God, and to hear a word that is not yours but God's. That takes style.

It is obvious in this passage that the word of God from Isaiah says that God is identified with the marginal people of life; therefore, one must lead the church to that place—and that can be tough.

In our tradition, nothing human is foreign to our religious faith—this is the message of the prophets of old. It must also be the message of the new prophets! You see, the agenda has not changed, only the arrangement of it.

To be a preacher today in The United Methodist Church and be indifferent to hot spots in various parts of the world, to the arms race, and to the plight of the world's majority—namely, the very poor—is to contradict the spirit of Isaiah and John Wesley—and your servant role as well. The crucible of human experience is the vessel in which our theology gets its identity. Our faith we get from scripture. Our theology we form through our encounter with God and God's world. "Fear not him who can kill the body, rather fear him who can kill your soul." Build that into your style. It is essential to servanthood.

A Gracenote

I must now add what Dr. Harrell Beck calls a gracenote, for I've laid quite a load on you and upon myself. To be a minister with rounded edges that do not break a bruised reed or extinguish a flickering wick require caring for the inner space that is you. Isaiah says of the servant's style, "He will not fail or be discouraged ..." But we do fail and we do become discouraged. How can we keep our servanthood intact?

A part of you is still with God. You will acquire that through your own way of prayer, reflection, and meditation. Many times after talking with disgruntled pastors, I realize they have become discouraged. In deeper consideration, I know that they have lost part of themselves. I think Isaiah is promising that God will give it back.

We have a clothes dryer that inhales socks—only one at a time. It doesn't get a chance at the other one because the other one doesn't get dirty anymore. It's tied in a knot in the drawer. I have enough single socks to outfit every one-legged man in Pulaski County. Socks are not very useful unless there is a pair.

We lose our effectiveness when a part of us is lost, or when there is a part of us we have never found—the part that God wants to give. Because of the promise of this scripture, apparently there is a part of us that resides with God. An effective style requires both parts.

I was working very late on a sermon the other night; pressure and deadline were weighing on me. I thought to myself: "Here I am hurrying in the darkness." Except for my activity, deep stillness prevailed. I thought: "Why hurry in the darkness? What a desecration of the gift of the night! Quiet voices nudge us into the reality of an existence beyond the pressures afforded by deadlines. Quiet is made for God to come out of hiding. Noise is a curtain which shuts out the whisper of God. Tension is a heavy form of energy that pushes back the divine dimension. Yet, all the while there is a Presence extending its hand, and I am too busy to reach out."

If I would, I could touch the part of myself that is missing. If I would, I could take time to extend my soul as invitation. I would find myself recharged and my call renewed.

Find your own time, your own way, your own subject matter, but know that God is; that God is in the moment of your longing and searching; that in every situation a saving possibility is there. A part of you is still with God. Prayer joins the parts so that you go on knowing God is holding your hand.

One day Charlie Brown and Lucy were leaning against a tree and Lucy says: "What do you think security is, Charlie Brown?" He says, " Security is sleeping in the back seat of the car when you're a little kid and you've been somewhere with your mom and dad, and it's night. You don't have to worry about anything. Your mom and dad are in the front seat, and they're doing all the worrying. They take care of everything." Lucy smiles and says, "That's real neat." But then Charlie begins to get a serious look on his face and raises his finger and says: "It doesn't last. Suddenly you're grown up, and it can never be that way again. Suddenly it's over, and you'll never get to sleep in the back seat again. Never!" Lucy gets a sad, frightened look on her face and says: "Never?" Charlie, devastated with the terrible truth he has spoken, replies: "Never." Lucy, stricken with this new knowledge of the real world, reaches over and says, "Hold my hand, Charlie Brown."

Be willing, find a place, a time, to say: "Hold my hand, Lord." He will give you that part of you that's needed. You will have style all right—and it will be adequate!

CHAPTER
12

To My Wife

Editor's note: In 1984, Ken Hicks was asked by the spouses of the ministers of the Arkansas Area of the United Methodist Church to write a tribute in honor of his wife on the occasion of their thirty-eighth wedding anniversary. That letter follows. As of this printing, Ken and Elaine have been married sixty-three years and counting.

Dear Elaine,

The occasion has arisen for me to wax eloquent. I've never been good at waxing anything, or sweeping, or mopping. But here I am, waxing eloquent.

I have to start by reminding myself that we have had nearly thirty-nine years together. I should hasten to say that the first of those thirty-nine was a year of courtship (to use a term slightly out of date).

As I recollect, the first time we saw each other was on an occasion when you were visiting the college campus. The event was along the theme of "Thanks for the Memories" or something of the sort. My lot was to be master of ceremonies in the role of Bob Hope. I've never really cared for Bob Hope, but I did the best I could to do him justice. Then later, you came to the same college to resume your studies after teaching school for a year.

You were a cute little dickens with eyes that twinkled like stars. I had no idea I could get a date with you, but I did and we've been at it ever since. Around Armistice Day of 1945 (no particular reason for that day) we went to Lincoln (Nebraska) to shop for an engagement ring. We found it—a stunning quarter carat diamond available on suitable terms.

I think it was along about then that we both got into trouble when we came back to the campus together with someone after my having played in a game of six-man football. We had only seven on the squad. I was supposed to come back with the team, but I came back with you instead. We were chastised.

When you had your appendix removed and had been out of the hospital just a few days, some of your dorm mates removed your mattress from your bed. On hearing about it, I charged upstairs shouting, "Man on second!" Girls scurried everywhere. The house-mother took me to task. I told her if it happened again, I would be back.

Then in August of 1946 we were married. The temperature was 110. I preached twice that morning. You got so excited at the wed-ding that you kissed the preacher instead of me after the ceremony.

Remember the '36 Chevy? Don Robinson had a '35. When we would meet while tooling around town, we would run into each other just for devilment. I spent all but $45.00 to get the thing in shape for our honeymoon. I gave your minister father $10.00 for marrying us. I thought he would give it back, but he didn't. So we had $35.00 with which to start for Colorado. The first evening the generator went bad. We limped into town where we were to spend the night with the knowledge that the car would have to be worked on the next morning.

We will always remember Pikes Peak. The old Chevy vapor locked about half way up and we had to coast down backward against the summer tourist traffic until we could pull off on the edge of the cliff. You got out to warn the traffic I was coming, and for your own safety. You were stunning in those shorts, especially when some kind people gave us a ride to the top where it was snowing.

There isn't time to recall the remainder of the honeymoon, except the remembrance that when we got to the home of relatives in Kansas after an all-night drive, we had fifty cents. Somehow we made it and we have been at it ever since.

The summer of '49 was a dilly. You were pregnant. We were in Denver. A year of seminary was behind us. I had a job at the packing plant. I didn't mind working on bacon, but when they put me on the killing floor I couldn't eat lunch.

Thank the Lord for the student appointment at Eads. So we went, not knowing where we were going. When we drove into that hot, dusty little town in eastern Colorado, there was that old basement church with weeds all around it. We parked down by the courthouse in the shade and cried together. But we were received with kindness. The sanctuary was built on the basement, and our first daughter was born. I finally got through seminary.

There have been so many times when tears turned to joy. There were the months of being apart all week while I was at school; times when the lack of clear divine guidance turned into providence across the years. The future has always been difficult to predict or foresee, but when we go someplace we find the Presence of God.

As I compose this piece, I find that so much must be omitted I did not realize was or has been or is part of our story. There have been bursts of grace which have revealed meaning in the small momentary revelations.

For instance, last August on our 37th anniversary, you will recall our going with family to a Mexican restaurant in Ovid, Colorado. Someone had the Mexican band play the Anniversary Waltz in our honor. Now, you know I can't dance. But in that restaurant full of people I got up, came to your chair and said, "Let's dance." And the look on your face, just for a moment was exactly that of the girl I asked to go to the movie on that first date thirty-eight years earlier. I was returned to another time by the assistance of the trumpet, two guitars, and a violin played Spanish style, and best of all, you. Fortunately, the place was crowded and there wasn't room to fall down.

Life is full of surprises both joyful and sad. But in the long haul, there is guidance and there is love. These are our moments of grace.

Many people have added to our blessing. For them we must both be grateful. This letter has prompted me to recollection, and this in itself has loosened a barrage of flashbacks which I had forgotten. Most have been left unwritten for lack of space. I would advise this exercise for others. And, had I not been asked I would not have known its therapy.

There is a journey which would have had no meaning had you not been there. The work of ministry and the task of living have too often buried the treasure of relationship. I'm sorry for that. For this, the request for forgiveness from you and our daughters is in order. But the longer the journey goes on the more carefully we watch the road signs. That is something that comes with seasoning, and seasoning takes time.

You are the seasoning of my years. Thanks for bearing the company of an imperfect husband and an imperfect church. Thank you for sharing the journey. There is more to come. Let's tell them all, "There is more to come." Love from the days of a '36 Chevy to this time is love come of age. You are not older. You are only better.

I can't imagine what they are going to do with this at the luncheon, but it should have been written anyhow and long ago. So put on your pumps and let's keep dancing. This time it will be my turn to tip the musicians.

Your husband and best friend,

Ken

AFTERWORD

One More Thought

I am asked occasionally, "Did you intend for retirement to be filled with so much activity?" The answer is "no." Prior to retirement I could see myself sitting in the back yard in the shade doing the reading I have always wanted to do. At noon Elaine would call me to lunch. Afterward, a nap would be in order and then I would do some more stuff of retirement.

The reality is this: since 1992, two things have happened. The first is that I had some invitations to serve in ways that would lead to new experiences outside the familiar church-fostered kind of things—Arkansas Advocates, Interfaith Caregiving (a national enterprise), and the Governor's Partnership Council for Children are examples.

Secondly, with the tragedy of 9/11 and ensuing events including war, it has become apparent to me that an intensity of faith enterprise is needed as a rethinking of our theology. Faith is not only about believing. It is also about intervention and advocacy and justice. People of faith and the people of America in general are generous and willing in doing deeds of mercy and goodness. When it comes to doing justice, we are timid and/or disagreeable. Justice is the challenge for now, and we don't do it well. As Father Camara of Brazil said, "When we feed the poor, we are called saints. When we ask, 'Why are so many poor and in poverty,' we are called communists."

This is the uncertainty and the unwillingness of our time. We have politicized our religion and theologized our politics. The result is fear, brashness, and deprivation. For me, it isn't a good time to succumb, surrender, or withdraw. That's my predicament. Where there is injustice and deprivation, that is where I think God dwells. "As you have done it to the least of these, you have done it to me." Somebody important said that once.

I heard this saying some time ago: If you're dancing with a bear, you don't get tired and sit down. You wait until the bear gets tired and then you sit down. Apparently for me, the bear is not yet tired.

KWH

Kenneth William Hicks

Kenneth William Hicks was born June 18, 1923, in southeastern Kansas, near Iola, into a farm family that attended Salem United Brethren Church, a country church that has existed for over one hundred years. Later in 1946, he would unite with The Methodist Church having served Methodist Churches as a student pastor.

Upon graduation from high school in 1941, Ken migrated to Nashville, Tennessee, to work in an airplane factory that built single-engine bombers. After a couple of years in this employment, a decision was made to relinquish his defense work and enter military service. A physical rejection notice engendered further consideration of preparation for ministry. After contending with family health issues for another year Kenneth began his studies by first attending a junior college, after which he enrolled at York College, a denominational school in York, Nebraska, graduating with a B.A. degree. Following this, he enrolled at Iliff School of Theology in Denver, Colorado, where he completed studies for a master of theology degree in 1953. Hicks's ordination track in The Methodist Church includes ordination as deacon in 1952 and as elder in 1953.

He served Methodist Churches in Colorado for a total of seven years. In 1955 Kenneth and his family moved to Nebraska to continue his ministry, which included five years in the position of district superintendent.

For Reverend Hicks the ministry he undertook was not a solitary one. He met his lovely wife, Elaine, during their collegiate years and their married life began in 1946. Since then they have been each other's counsel in all matters.

Election to The United Methodist Episcopacy occurred in 1976 at the Jurisdictional Conference held in Lincoln, Nebraska. At the time Hicks was senior pastor of Trinity United Methodist Church in Grand Island, Nebraska. He was assigned the Arkansas Area comprised of the Little Rock Conference and the North Arkansas

Conference (the two conferences were merged in 2002 to become what is presently the Arkansas Conference). During his service in Arkansas he established an excellent record of credibility and gained a respectable reputation for leadership in human relations, justice issues, and a respect for life. He also garnered a significant amount of publicity when he was called as a plaintiff to testify against the legislation that would have allowed creation science to be taught in public schools, the product of state legislation signed by Governor Frank White. The federal trial judge decided against the constitutionality of the law and it was repealed.

After eight years in Arkansas Bishop Hicks was assigned to the Kansas Episcopal Area, which included the Kansas East and Kansas West Conferences. Again he served for a very enlightening eight years, prodding and challenging the pastors, district superintendents, and laity in his care to innovative and effective approaches to ministry. Once again, publicity seemed to follow his shadow when a Kansas church-affiliated hospital came into a negotiated sale arrangement to a private corporate entity. Though he walked into the developing stages of this sale in his first months in Kansas, he was the one who presided over the consummation of a matter seething with controversy. The hospital is still operating under the name Wesley Hospital, and two significant health ministry foundations exist to foster healthy lives in Kansas. After retirement, Hicks served on the board of Kansas Health Foundation for eleven years.

In 1992 after sixteen years of mentoring United Methodists in two states, Ken and his wife retired back to Arkansas, where he was given an office in Little Rock's Pulaski Heights United Methodist Church as bishop in residence. Since his arrival in retirement, he has had little time to live out retirement because his services are always in demand and his commitment to issues and causes close to his heart continue to beckon.

Hicks has been granted five honorary degrees by the following schools: from Nebraska Wesleyan University, Lincoln, Nebraska; Westmar College, LeMars, Iowa; Philander Smith College, Little Rock, Arkansas; Hendrix College, Conway, Arkansas; and Baker

University, Baldwin, Kansas. He has also served on the board of trustees at the latter three of the above-listed schools plus St. Paul School of Theology at Kansas City, Kansas; Southwestern University at Winfield, Kansas; Kansas Wesleyan University at Salinas, Kansas; and Southern Methodist University in Dallas, Texas. He has also served as a trustee for Mount Sequoyah Assembly in Fayetteville, Arkansas; Youthville Inc. at Newton, Kansas; Lydia Patterson Institute at El Paso, Texas; Methodist Hospital at Memphis, Tennessee; and Friendly Acres Retirement Center in Newton, Kansas. Whew!

The service record of Ken Hicks during his active ministry includes membership on the General Board of Church and Society, and General Board of Global Ministries being chair of the National Division of that agency for four of the eight years of service with Global ministries. Committee chairmanships on these two boards included Peace with Justice and Chair of the Advisory Committee on Korean Ministry. Committees on the boards he served included responsibilities to Nicaragua, El Salvador, Brazil, and Korea. There is more to his record, but this book has to end somewhere.

Since retirement, Ken Hicks has served or is now serving as a member of Arkansas Friends for Better Schools, Arkansas Advocates for Children and Families, Governor's Partnership Council for Children and Families, Advisory Council of Carelink (Area Agency on Aging), Advisory Council of Friends of Research in Psychiatry (UAMS), Interfaith Caregivers Alliance, Board of Kansas Health Foundation, Bishops' Initiative on Children and Poverty, and the Arkansas Coalition to Abolish the Death Penalty. Throw in being a docent at the Clinton Presidential Library and a member of the Steering Committee of Arkansas Interfaith Power and Light, a movement gaining national recognition in advocating for care of the world. Can you see why he cannot truly call himself retired?

Among his many awards he was presented with the Civil Libertarian of the Year by the ACLU-Arkansas in 1984; the Senator David Pryor Award in 1997 for Community Service by CareLink; the Ethel K. Miller Award for Religion and Social Awareness by Hendrix College in 1999; and he and Elaine received the Hospice

Foundation of Arkansas Compassion Award in 1999. "Unselfish and devoted community leadership" describes the Hazo Carter Jr. Presidential Award from Philander Smith College. He also received the Distinguished Alumnus Award from Iliff School of Theology. There obviously have been many more, but for the sake of not cutting down an enormously large number of additional trees, these should suffice.

For several years Hicks has been a part-time director of Ministries of Methodist Family Health. His is a ministry for troubled and uprooted children and youth, including a behavioral hospital, numerous care centers around the state, and ministry for moms with addictions who have their children with them. This is a ministry of high-quality and credentialed care.

Most recently, Bishop Hicks has been heavily involved in leadership of the Peace Ministry of the Pulaski Heights United Methodist Church. This program began in 2002 to "serve as a faith-focused, community-centered resource for personal and group education, exploration, and experience in the areas of peacemaking and reconciliation." It is supported by the church and the Little Rock community and by the Bishop Kenneth W. Hicks Peace Endowment maintained by the Pulaski Heights United Methodist Foundation (which will benefit from sales of this book).

And, of course, no biography of Kenneth and Elaine Hicks would be complete without mentioning that they are proud parents of two very accomplished daughters, Linda Hicks and Debra Gottschalk, who is married to Wayne Gottschalk, and are the parents of Ken and Elaine's very special grandchildren: Kiley and Spencer.

Shalom!

TTTT